HORIZON

JANUARY, 1962   ·   VOLUME IV, NUMBER 3

HORIZON
A Magazine of the Arts

JANUARY, 1962 · *VOLUME IV, NUMBER 3*

PUBLISHER
James Parton

EDITORIAL DIRECTOR
Joseph J. Thorndike, Jr.

EDITOR
William Harlan Hale

MANAGING EDITOR
Eric Larrabee

ASSOCIATE EDITOR
Ralph Backlund

ASSISTANT EDITORS
Ada Pesin
Jane Wilson

CONTRIBUTING EDITOR
Margery Darrell

EDITORIAL ASSISTANTS
Shirley Abbott, Caroline Backlund
Wendy Buehr, Alan Doré, Charles L. Mee, Jr.

COPY EDITOR
Mary Ann Pfeiffer
Assistants: Joan Rehe, Ruth H. Wolfe

ART DIRECTOR
Irwin Glusker
Associate Art Director: Elton Robinson

ADVISORY BOARD
Gilbert Highet, *Chairman*
Frederick Burkhardt   Oliver Jensen
Marshall B. Davidson   Jotham Johnson
Richard M. Ketchum   John Walker

EUROPEAN CONSULTING EDITOR
J. H. Plumb
Christ's College, Cambridge

EUROPEAN BUREAU
Gertrudis Feliu, *Chief*
28 Quai du Louvre, Paris

HORIZON is published every two months by American Heritage Publishing Co., Inc. Executive and editorial offices: 551 Fifth Ave., New York 17, N.Y. HORIZON welcomes contributions but can assume no responsibility for unsolicited material.

All correspondence about subscriptions should be addressed to: HORIZON Subscription Office, 379 West Center St., Marion, Ohio.

Single Copies: $4.50
Annual Subscriptions: $21.00 in the U.S. & Can.
$22.00 elsewhere

An annual index is published every September, priced at $1. HORIZON is also indexed in the *Readers Guide to Periodical Literature.*

Title registered U.S. Patent Office
Second-class postage paid at New York, N.Y.

COVER: What mysterious portent has filled the Delphic Sibyl's wide-set eyes with wonder and apprehension? We do not know, for at the moment of revelation she was transfixed forever on the ceiling of the Sistine Chapel and thus became part of the world's most famous work of art. She is perhaps the most beautiful of the five pagan sibyls that Michelangelo incorporated in his stupendous fresco to symbolize pre-Christian intimations of divine truth. Although the Sistine ceiling provides the overwhelming experience of any visit to the Vatican, it is only one of the marvels in that tiny state-within-a-city. Many of these are described in an article by Alfred Werner beginning on page 22, which is accompanied by a portfolio of Vatican treasures printed by Skira.

FRONTISPIECE: This remarkably animated version of Stone Age life was produced without benefit of Darwin, Alley Oop, or *The Flintstones*, all of whom it anticipates by four to five hundred years. The fifteenth-century artist who painted it was not, however, actually trying to portray our ancestors (whom he unhesitatingly would have put in the Garden of Eden), but rather the benighted inhabitants of Cedar, *"région d'Orient."* Just who he was we do not know, except that he worked as an illuminator for the parents of Francis I. His cave-man drama is one of the many lively miniatures with which he decorated a naïve manuscript of travel and description, *Secrets de l'Histoire Naturelle,* sometime between 1480 and 1500. None has been reproduced in this country before.

*As director of the Ford Founda-
tion's program in the Humanities
and Arts, W. McNeil Lowry (left)
spreads his largesse wide. A sam-
pling: opposite, Ford-supported
repertory actors at the Alley Theatre in Houston, Texas; below,
printing a lithograph at the Ford-
backed Tamarind Workshop in
Los Angeles; opposite below, Norman Dello Joio rehearsing his new
Ford-sponsored opera* Blood Moon.

Pouring in little money so far but much

Of all the Children's Crusades that have set out to make the
world perfect in our time, the biggest, best-financed, and
most childlike was that of the Ford Foundation. On its
emergence from a limited family fund into a "national philanthropy" in 1950, the Foundation had total assets of something over two billion dollars (depending on the value assigned to the Ford Motor Company stock, which was then
privately held and had no market price). This money was
to be devoted in its entirety to improving the quality of
human behavior, in education and in political, economic,
and international relations. The order of the day was,
Straight Ahead; and for years the children marched, only
to be beset by misadventures and to lose much gold in the
sands. They were ambushed by barbarians from the Congress, Turks from the press, Byzantines from the universities;
Congressman Carroll Reece pursued their Robert M. Hutchins with an investigation, and Henry Ford II, who had sent
them off, donned sackcloth and declared Hutchins's Fund
for the Republic a "wholly disowned subsidiary."

Inevitably, the commanders who had to live with such

FORD MOVES IN ON THE ARTS

By MARTIN MAYER

energy, the Foundation is busy priming creative pumps across the land

disappointments began to feel a need for other approaches and other worlds to conquer. Some of these were orthodox: there were wide grants to hospitals and the sciences. Then, finally, after two years of preparation, the Foundation struck out again toward uncertain goals through treacherous territory: the arts. Since 1957 it has appropriated two or three million dollars every year under a program it names "Humanities and the Arts"—aid to university presses, libraries, "humanistic scholarship," new painting, sculpture, theater, opera, musical composition, novel writing, poetry, etc. The money goes out in closely supervised, separate projects, most of which expire within two years; the 1962 program, approved by the Board of Trustees last September, involves seven projects of which only three continue previous Ford endeavors in the same field. Yet, though the outlay may seem small, its range is phenomenal, extending from carefully weighed subsidies to poets in Brooklyn to the commissioning of new theater ventures in Texas and the publishing of monographs of abstract painters on the West Coast.

The decision to move in on the arts was by no means an easy one for Ford's trustees to make. Their initial frame of reference had excluded any possibility of help to artists. They were serious men—business executives and college presidents (assuming some difference between these two categories)—and the arts are after all frivolities, exalted forms of entertainment and recreation. If you give the Committee for Economic Development $525,000 to do a study of national monetary policy, you have a thick, satisfyingly exportable document to read when you are done. If you give Leon Kirchner $4,000 to write a piano concerto for Leon Fleisher to perform, you get a piano concerto which cannot possibly influence the price of cocoa in Ghana and which few, if any, of the trustees would greatly care to hear.

What convinced the trustees, apparently, was the argument that the arts are in fact more than an embellishment —they are a phenomenon of behavior that can profitably be studied. In setting up what is known around the Ford shop as the "H/A" program, the trustees in 1957 charged their personnel, first, "to prepare over several years a comprehensive study of the economic and social positions of the

artist and of his institutions in the United States today."
Actual grants to the arts could thus be justified as experiment: one can always learn more about an existing situation by disturbing it and then observing the precipitates. It is a measure of the quality of the people who have run this program that the original dull goal of just another survey has virtually been ignored: despite the piling up of field reports, "interview diaries," statistical evidence, and flamboyant opinion, the "comprehensive study" is now further from completion than it was in 1957. William McPeak, of the Ford executive echelon, says that if H/A now wants to forget the study, it's okay with the Foundation.

Though H/A is the largest organized foundation program in the arts (and the only one to do anything beyond helping institutions and individuals to carry out their own plans), it is in Ford terms a very small effort. Less than 2 per cent of the Ford budget is allocated to it, and not all of that is available for the arts (a fraction goes through universities, like most of Ford's money). H/A occupies only one corner of one of the eight floors Ford fills at 477 Madison Avenue in New York, and its staff was only recently increased to a grand total of five persons (plus secretaries). But this tiny program accounts for about half the mail received by the Foundation, and its publicity rivals that of the Ford Fund for the Advancement of Education, which puts most of its energies into procuring publicity for its goals.

Most important, H/A has shown results. At the least, it has produced some music, some paintings and sculpture, some novels, some theatrical productions, that might not have existed without Ford's help. W. McNeil Lowry, the program's director, admits (or claims, depending on his auditors) that H/A can be no more than "a finger in the dike" against the sea of troubles battering at the arts in America. "With two or three million dollars a year, we aren't going to change trends." The British socialist R. H. S. Crossman, however, once put postwar Europe's problem in an aphorism: "When the United States sneezes, Europe gets pneumonia." Ford's sneeze in the direction of the arts could greatly influence the vitality of a community that lives forever at the margin of its resources. And H/A has already shown—in projects that assign young composers to high-school orchestras, that provide year-long contracts for pro-

One of Ford's most ambitious projects is to commission new theater designs for our day, thereby bringing fresh thinking to bear upon an old subject. Opposite is the model of a theater for modern dance—one of eight different schemes for houses for various contemporary purposes, being placed on exhibition this month in New York under Ford auspices and soon to tour the nation. In this design by Barrie Greenbie, Elizabeth Harris, and Seth Hiller, the stage is octagonal, with adjustable ramps and platforms for flexibility. The 1,100 seat auditorium lets the audience surround and look down on the dancers. An orchestra could be hidden above the stage.

fessional actors at regional theaters, or that purchase paintings, sculptures, and prints for regional museums—a quality of initiative and imagination very rare among those who foot the bills for art.

"Ford," says "Mac" Lowry in one of his rare pompous moments, "started out as a problem-oriented foundation; then it became a subject-matter foundation, like all the others." Lowry lived through the transition, not always happily. He had started as an academic with a Ph.D. in English literature, teaching at the University of Illinois; after the war, he became Washington correspondent for the Cox newspapers and then an officer of the International Press Institute in Zurich. He came to Ford in 1953 to work in its education program and two years later took over its program of grants to the "humanities." It was his relentless urging that persuaded the officers of the Foundation to broaden his program to include humanities *and* the arts. Since March, 1957, Lowry has been a wanderer on the face of the earth. He has visited about fifty American communities to look over the artistic terrain (his staff has covered another 110), and he probably knows more than anyone else in America about the functioning of the European tax-supported "arts councils."

Ford's H/A does not accept other people's definitions of the problems of the arts. Lowry and his staff find their own targets and then, hopefully, find weapons to aim at the targets. Naturally, they use silver bullets—but Lowry has only a limited faith in the magical properties of money alone. By order of the trustees (probably at Lowry's urging) H/A is barred from making grants to institutions for capital or general operating expenses: each grant must be to a specific individual or for a specific purpose. Lowry has also refused to devote himself to talent hunts, to the endless examination of straws from the haystack of the arriving generation. "We could do it," he says, "but we'd be a drop in the bucket next to the Fulbright program." From a group of young painters, nearly all of whom had already received Fulbrights, Lowry heard the horrible phrase "grant goon" used to describe the ardent spirit who lives by sucking gifts from the government and voluntary organizations. The words stuck, and one of Lowry's many fears is that Ford money will be wasted on yet another attempt to insulate beginning artists from the cold winds of the real world, which they must eventually enter.

With a few exceptions, then, Lowry's problems are those which afflict recognized talents who have demonstrated a high order of ability (and who have probably already received at least one grant from somebody), but whose artistic production seems to be hindered by economic forces beyond their control. "Most people who have any talent at all, unless they're bone idle, are using it successfully," says Alan Pryce-Jones, former editor of the Literary Supplement of the *Times* of London, who looked over the American arts scene on a grant from Ford and then joined Lowry's staff in the spring of 1961. But in most of the arts rude economic interference appears to prevent people from working as successfully as they might, once their first flights of youth are past. Most of Lowry's projects have attempted to find out how much more successfully these already "successful" artists could work in an improved economic atmosphere.

Ford's program, during its first four years, explored and applied poultices of money to several inflamed areas, including the following:

CREATIVE WRITING (novels and poetry). The problem here is that of insufficient income for time expended. Three or four years of work will produce—for poetry, certainly, and for serious novels, almost certainly—less money than a schoolteacher's annual salary. Thus, most writers have to teach or lecture in order to make a living, and these activities may (or may not) interfere with their writing. To writers, Ford has granted eleven two-year fellowships of up to $8,500 a year. (According to need, which has to be demonstrated to Lowry personally, the average grant has been about $6,500 a year.) The recipients have included such figures as James Baldwin, Saul Bellow, e. e. cummings, Bernard Malamud, Flannery O'Connor, and Katherine Anne Porter. They all needed the money, though the reasons for the need must have varied greatly: as the advertising business has so vigorously demonstrated, economic "needs" are a function of a life style.

GRAPHIC AND PLASTIC ARTS. Here the problem is one of absolute insufficiency of income; one recipient of a Ford grant in this project said that he ate salt for nourishment the week before his good fortune was announced.

Lowry looked over a sample of twenty artists who sold paintings through recognized dealers in 1958; their average net income, including income from teaching, ran about $5,000 a year after deduction of dealers' commissions and costs of supplies. Income taxation has held down prices for all artists whose names are not big enough to make the ownership of their work look like a hedge against inflation. Museums—even well-endowed "major" ones—characteristically have only a tiny purchase budget and must scrounge money from charitable friends for each item they wish to buy. Nationwide reputations, moreover, are hard to come by: a book is published and distributed nationally, a musical score is available for performance anywhere, but a painting or sculpture stays where it is unless the money is put up to move it.

Ford tackled, or at least slapped the pants of all these problems. In 1957–1961 twenty painters and sculptors were given grants of $10,000 each (everybody got $10,000, and many of the artists spread the money over three years because they couldn't imagine what they'd do with that much cash in one year). Twenty-one others were awarded "purchase prizes"—that is, they were authorized to donate a work to a local museum, school, library, or college, and Ford paid them for it at an average price of about $650. Nineteen more were given retrospective exhibitions of their work, opening in their local area with handsome catalogues to distribute, and then traveling around the country under the auspices of the American Federation of Arts. Here again, a number of the names were well-known: Abraham Rattner, Milton Avery, Andrew Dasburg, Lee Gatch, Karl Zerbe.

In 1962 Ford will seek to buttress still more solidly the

One of 16 Ford composers now in residence at U. S. high schools, Robert Muczynski hears a trio play what he has written for it.

reputations of living American artists by sponsoring the publication of a series of monographs devoted to their work; the recipients of these professional puffs have not yet been chosen. Another new project will greatly expand the "purchase prize" award, with prices up to $6,000 for a sculpture and $4,500 for a painting, the work to be donated, as before, to a local art center.

MUSIC. The composer's problems are competition from the past, plus the short end of the division of labor. Few people would claim to be seriously interested in art without having some interest in living painters, but many musicians spend their entire musical life with the compositions of previous generations. And today's composers are the first in history to try to make a living from their writing (except for the writers of Italian operas, composers used to live off careers as executant artists or, occasionally, as teachers and critics). But the new Mozarts, Mahlers, and Prokofievs do not perform, any more than the Paganinis of our time compose. Worse yet, where a composer could once guarantee the performance of his music by playing it himself, he must now (unless he is Leonard Bernstein) approach third parties, most of whom are more interested in developing their own interpretations of past music. Well-known composers can get *first* performances fairly easily, because a conductor thereby receives the distinction of a world première. Subsequent performances, however, are hard to secure, and younger composers may go for years without hearing a note of their own orchestral music.

So II/A has bluntly paid for performances. Among its first grants, in 1957, was one to the American Music Center, which arranged with six symphony orchestras—Boston, Knoxville, Minneapolis, Oklahoma City, San Francisco, and Washington—to commission one work each for the three following years and to play each year at least three of the works commissioned by the others. (Boston eventually backed out and was replaced by Rochester.) Later, H/A arranged for prominent performers—people of the top rank but not yet household names, like the pianist Leon Fleisher, the violinists Joseph Fuchs and Michael Rabin, the sopranos Adele Addison and Phyllis Curtin—to commission works for themselves, with orchestra, from composers of their choice. Each of the artists performed the resulting work with three orchestras, the list here being Atlanta, Denver, Houston, Indianapolis, Los Angeles, New York, Pittsburgh, San Antonio, and Seattle. Ford paid each artist $5,000 to cover performing fees and traveling expenses, each composer a $3,000 commission plus up to $1,000 for copying of parts, and each orchestra $3,000 for the extra rehearsals involved in new music. The composers represented make virtually a house register of known American talent, particularly in the middle-age range where the list includes Elliott Carter, Lukas Foss, Leon Kirchner, and Ben Weber.

In the music area, too, Ford has granted moneys to unknown youngsters. A remarkably imaginative scheme, suggested by the composer Norman Dello Joio and administered by the National Music Council, has in the past four years sent about forty young composers, at Ford expense, into public school systems throughout the United States to serve as "composers in residence." There, for the high-school orchestras, choruses, and bands, they write everything from concert pieces for assemblies, to marches for the football field. Another grant to younger talent in music involves a project to train conductors to know professional musicians and the standard repertory. This plan, administered by Baltimore's Peabody Conservatory, will use men from the Baltimore Symphony and such visiting artists as Fritz Reiner, George Szell, and Alfred Wallenstein.

THEATER. The challenge here is most grimly revealed in the continuing argument between those who believe the theater is dead and those who believe it is merely in a catatonic trance. "We don't have theater," says Alan Schneider, a young recipient of a Ford grant who directs off Broadway and in regional theaters; "we put on shows." The Broadway theater has lost much of the audience that was worth having and now depends largely on the goodwill of some brisk Helen Hokinson ladies who organize theater parties. Off-Broadway theater lives in large part as an expensive advertising medium for the people who participate in it: the actors often leave a production as soon as they can after the reviews and go looking for walk-on parts in television, which may pay seven times as much for one brief appearance as the off-Broadway stage pays for a week's work. Outside New York the theater lives on confessedly amateur university productions in new, well-equipped auditoriums, essentially amateur local repertory companies in converted grain pits, and road versions of the latest Broadway cyc-wash in former vaudeville houses.

Ford, shuddering slightly, turned its back on New York (over-the-shoulder grants were given to New York's Phoenix Theatre and to a few off-Broadway directors, among them the admirable Alvin Epstein). The effort has been to build an audience for theater outside New York and to provide better theater in the few places where interest already exists. One of the first Ford grants ($136,000) went to the Cleveland Play House for a professional touring company. Later, grants of $10,000 each went to some twenty directors, mostly out of town, who could use the money to "enrich their artistic development" (i.e., by travel, typically to the Berliner Ensemble, Vilar's TNP, Joan Littlewood's Theatre Royal in London, and Tyrone Guthrie's showcase in Stratford, Ontario), or to improve the quality of their own productions by hiring professionals whose services they could not otherwise afford. A subsequent program made larger grants to Houston's Alley Theatre, Washington's Arena Stage, San Francisco's Actor's Workshop, and New York's Phoenix, to enable them to hire actors for a season at a guaranteed salary of $200 a week and thereby be free of the curse of "the jobbing actor" who comes and goes.

At first, Ford thought the problem of finding playwrights could be solved merely by paying for productions. A hunt was made for ten unproduced plays to be performed under subsidy at regional and university theaters; the first time around, eight plays were accepted, but on the second go-round the judges found only four. "We became very discouraged," Lowry says, "about the quality of the people who already called themselves playwrights." The result was a project that gathered in eleven novelists and poets and "tried to bait them into an interest in the theater" by paying them to spend a year just hanging around a stage. The eleven included such accomplished writers as the poets Robert Lowell and Richard Wilbur, the novelists Herbert Gold, Mark Harris, James Purdy, and Peter Taylor. It is hoped that some of them will someday write plays or librettos.

Still other Ford projects have tried to modernize American theater production, which has scarcely advanced since the days of Belasco. One project gave grants to seven pairs of architects and designers (and Frederick Kiesler, who is both) to produce blueprints and models of theaters that would either suit specific forms—modern dance, "intimate music drama," outdoor summer production—or would be flexible to the needs of a new generation of nonrealist playwrights. Sketches and models of these new theaters will be toured around the country throughout 1962, under Ford auspices, in hopes that the universities and community groups now planning to build theaters will take heed—and in the somewhat more distant hope of holding Broadway's feet to the fire. Another project will enable regional theaters to commission sets and sculpture from local artists, to give their productions greater visual integrity than can usually be achieved by the hard-pressed, often part-time, permanent "designer" on the staff. Yet another, to be launched next year, will seek to train young managers who can take the "front" worries off the bowed shoulders of the driving or driven optimists who struggle to maintain repertory theaters, civic operas, and orchestras in the American hinterland.

OPERA. The most complicated and expensive of collaborative art forms, opera in America has suffered grievously from the lack of an informing tradition, yet American artists have done better in this field than in any other during the years since the war. Unfortunately, they have had to go abroad to reap the rewards of their incredibly good training. Ford has gambled here in two directions: it has sponsored new American operas in hopes of interesting an audience and starting a tradition, and it has subsidized regional opera houses to give experience in major roles to young singers who could not yet hope for such a chance at the Metropolitan Opera, or in Chicago, Dallas, or San Francisco.

To serve the first of these goals, the New York City Opera has produced, under Ford subsidy, no fewer than eighteen American operas and taken five of them on tour as far west as St. Louis. A subsequent grant (totaling $950,-000) will permit the Metropolitan, the New York City Opera, Chicago, and San Francisco to commission and produce world premières of eighteen new American operas; the first four, by Norman Dello Joio, Vittorio Giannini, Douglas Moore, and Robert Ward, were heard last fall. To serve the second goal, H/A gave one of its first grants to Renato

JOE MONROE—LENSGROUP

Four American operas sponsored by Ford premièred last fall.
Here Mary Costa rehearses Blood Moon *in San Francisco.*

Cellini's New Orleans Opera for a scheme that presented young American singers as Madame Butterfly rather than as Kate Pinkerton. From 1962 to 1965 Ford will give thirty additional singers such opportunities, in New Orleans and elsewhere (but not in New York, Chicago, or San Francisco). Ford will pay the young singers' fees and expenses, relieving the opera company of all financial obligations, and will give each of the artists chosen $2,500 to cover the costs of learning new roles, studying acting, etc.

ACADEMIC INFLUENCE. During the last generation—but particularly in the years since World War II—colleges and universities have increasingly become the major income source for the arts in America. The John Simon Guggenheim Foundation recently took note of the fact that more and more of its fellowships in the arts were going to people with university affiliations but found on examination that nothing could be done: nearly all the applications were coming in from people at universities.

This may be the most important problem of all, for it *does* matter where the money comes from. The universities do influence fashions of acceptability in art; they promote easily analyzed sterility—the poem written for the New Critic, the symbolist novel, the abstract expressionist painting, the twelve-tone or electronic composition. Great works of art have been produced in each of these forms (except electronic music), but the major reason for their dominance is probably the fact that the university professor can analyze them without embarrassing references to the visceral qualities of art. He can also teach the rationalized technique so successfully that many of his pupils will be able to pour out formally correct mediocrity and thence move on to their own teaching careers. Because future income is so likely to arrive from the smooth hands of a university treasurer, the young artist is strongly tempted to study his craft within ivied walls rather than in the grubby atmosphere of the art school or the conservatory; and there is more than a little reason to believe that the sort of "general education" offered at most American colleges and universities actually inhibits the production of art.

Lowry does not talk happily about this problem (he has to live with universities, too), but he obviously regards the academic influence on the arts as essentially pernicious. (When a dramatist is nominated for a grant with the words, "Mr. X has had a very rich academic life pointed toward a career in playwrighting and activity in the theater since 1951," something is very wrong.) This trend is almost the definition of what Lowry cannot hope to change with his limited budget: indeed, the gigantism of academia fits so neatly into so many other American trends that no amount of money would be likely to remedy it. In a small way, however, H/A has struck some blows for liberty. One of its first grants was to the Minneapolis Society of Fine Arts—$150,000 for an experiment in curriculum design which might give the art schools some means of competing against

the universities. Another project (twice repeated in later years) awarded grants to people expressly *not* affiliated with universities—conductors, architects, museum curators, etc. —for "studies in the creative arts." Many Ford grants have been given to relieve artists of the necessity to teach. Where recipients have asked whether they might continue to work with their own pupils, H/A has replied that this was their own business; where they have asked whether they could continue to teach even part time at a university, H/A has asked them to cease and desist.

All H/A projects start in roughly the same way. Lowry and his staff circulate around the country, listening carefully and looking at the local situation. "For most people," Lowry says, "it's the first time a foundation ever came to see *them*." The staff then checks its impressions with "consultants"—privately, over lunch tables or telephone wires—and develops descriptions of the problems with ideas for grants. These "consultants" include virtually everybody whose name has ever been publicly connected to the art in question. About twenty of them are then summoned to New York, to sit around a vast coffin-shaped table in Ford's eighteenth-floor mausoleum (complete with wax plants). If possible, they are paid nothing but travel expenses, though Lowry will grudgingly pony up $50 a day if he must; H/A is very tight with Ford's money.

Conversation at the table is general and occasionally spirited; Lowry, by letting out a notch on his controlled but considerable native impatience, can usually avoid *ad hominem* arguments. At most of the meetings specific projects will be suggested, either by a consultant or by Lowry; at a good meeting ideas will be flung about, puffed and deflated, embellished and simplified, perhaps even made ready for practical staff work. A number of apparently attractive but actually harebrained schemes—for example, a project to subsidize "little" magazines to create economically significant markets for advanced imaginative writing—have been buried at these conferences.

At this point Lowry and his staff draw up what looks like a workable way to spend the money and circularize their plan both to the participants in the conference and to some eminent outsiders. Comments from all sources are considered, modifications made, and the resulting "docket item" passed on first to the Foundation's senior officers and then to the trustees—"my trustees," as Lowry says. "None of these projects even exists until my trustees have approved it."

Generally people become eligible for H/A grants through nomination by third parties rather than through their own application. (An exception to this rule was the contest for playwrights who wished to have their plays produced at the regional theaters; they were allowed to submit scripts to the New Dramatists Committee—itself a Rockefeller creation—for possible recommendation to the ultimate jury.) Nominations are solicited from literally hundreds of "pro-

11

fessionals" in the field where the grants are to be awarded. Nearly 500 writers, editors, and university people made nominations of novelists and poets for fellowships; nearly 900 painters, sculptors, print makers, museum directors, and teachers nominated for the first of the art programs.

Nominees are now asked whether or not they would wish to be considered for a grant; if they like the idea, they fill out a "submission form," and a "statement of purpose." Names of nominees then go to a jury—three jurors in the visual arts projects, usually five in the others, once as many as seven. The jurors look at the paintings (hung in a warehouse) or read the plays or books or listen to tapes and read scores of compositions, and then make their decisions without interference from the H/A staff, which may, however, sit in on the deliberations.

With the exception of the jury that chose young composers for high-school orchestras, all Ford juries have been anonymous. This policy is not unique—the Guggenheim Foundation gives its music fellowships on the decision of an anonymous jury, though the names of the art jurors are made public—but it is obviously susceptible to abuse, and some people resent it bitterly. Many who dislike it in theory, however, will accept it in practice—"Everybody knows," says the artist Gabor Peterdi, "that, assuming you have any friends, the best way to lose 99 per cent of them is to serve on a jury." Members of the Guggenheim art jury have pleaded with that foundation's secretary general, Henry Allen Moe, to be excused from future service on just these grounds. Lowry, of course, would never hear such pleas: as a matter of policy, each H/A juror serves once only.

The names of H/A's jurors are a well-kept secret, but the range and caliber of its consultants (see sample panels on page 14) indicate that by and large, Lowry's choice of advisers has been imaginative and strikingly well-balanced. All major schools are represented on most Ford juries, and where possible a swing-man of idiosyncratic tastes has been found. People who have observed the deliberations of both Ford and Guggenheim juries feel that the outside world worries too much about doctrinaire or fanatic jurors: because he is choosing an artist for purposes of recognition rather than a particular work for a prize, they say, the responsible juror casts aside most of his prejudices of style and taste and judges only the technical mastery, the developed craftsmanship of the candidate. However they work, Lowry's juries have come up with mixed bags of winners. The level of quality has been high, too. A man who has been closely involved with several arts, and who hates foundations, says, "I don't know people the Ford Foundation has given money to that I wouldn't give money to."

The "success" of Ford awards is impossible to measure objectively. Art is, by its nature, an immensely wasteful occupation. From any period's art works, only a handful survives, and value is inevitably judged by survival. "That which is only living," as T. S. Eliot once put it, "can only die." The H/A staff is very modest in its claims. "If you get a one or two per cent return," says Marcia Thompson, the indispensable organizer of H/A's machinery, "you've done quite well."

Ford's most obviously successful project has been that in which musical performers commissioned new works for solo-

CHIC LLOYD

Under a Ford project to assist new playwrights, Sidney Michaels's Plaster Bambino *is played in San Francisco with the Broadway star Burgess Meredith.*

12

ist and orchestra. The average was astonishingly good, and one of the pieces—Lukas Foss's *Time Cycle*, written for Adele Addison—won the New York Critics Circle Prize for the 1960–61 season. The opera projects are far too young to be either a success or a failure. The art projects, in the opinion of artists, are *comme ci comme ça*. One of the artists who received a retrospective exhibition wrote Ford that he was delighted with the results because he had afterward sold more paintings at higher prices, which, to be wholly practical, makes the grant for his show a success. Others probably did less well; a New York museum officer feels that the "extreme grass-roots approach" to the art awards (the insistence on going after artists outside New York) made some of them ineffective. This, of course, is a New Yorker's opinion.

There has also been criticism in New York of Ford's high concentration on regional theaters. They have not developed new acting styles, production techniques, playwrights, or (with the possible exception of San Francisco's Actor's Workshop) sophisticated audiences. "The only contribution these theaters have made so far," says a man who has worked in them and believes in them, "is their existence." But we live in a period when we can scarcely afford to sneer at mere existence. It seems generally agreed that the grants to Nina Vance's Alley Theatre in Houston, Zelda Fichandler's Arena Stage in Washington, and John Reich's Goodman Memorial Theatre in Chicago helped produce at least some first-class theater. ("If I had ten more like Nina and Zelda," Lowry says, "I could plant ten more theaters anywhere in the United States.") It also seems generally agreed that the dozen plays produced with Ford subsidy were mostly pretty bad, and theater people feel that Ford will be lucky if one of the eminent novelists and poets assigned to live with a theater actually turns out a stageable play.

H/A has been pommeled by the newspapers only once, when the Metropolitan Opera commissioned with Ford money an opera from Marc Blitztein, whose political opinions are not precisely those of William Randolph Hearst, Jr. Blitztein chose as his subject the Sacco-Vanzetti case, and the post office began to empty bags of mail about the head of Henry Heald, president of the Foundation: "I am sure you would not wish to see Henry Ford's money go to the glorification of these anarchist murderers, etc." (One correspondent, more sophisticated historically, deplored the idea even though "Mr. Ford himself always believed they were innocent.") This brouhaha actually had nothing to do with Ford, which had merely given the money to the Met, but some difficulty was experienced in persuading Rudolph Bing that the Met's announcement should clarify the question of who was responsible for what. "Sacco and Vanzetti," says a man who spoke with Bing at that time—"so far as Bing was concerned, it was something out of the Italian Renaissance, like Guelphs and Ghibellines. He couldn't see what the fuss was about."

Lowry has soured somewhat on the straight fellowship which gives an artist money "without changing his relation to his environment." It is by no means proved that people on these grants do *even as much* work as they might do on top of routine teaching assignments or the like. "We operate," says the sculptress Hilda Morris, "in a kind of inertia. The grant makes another kind of inertia. It frees you to be creative, not only in a good sense, but also in an ungood sense." At the same time Lowry has become suspicious of "regranting" projects that give money to a trade association of the arts and let the association run the show. At present Lowry is willing to undertake the labor of "hand polishing" grants to individuals for fairly specific purposes, with institutions playing a subsidiary role. "Is this the way a foundation should work?" Lowry asks rhetorically and replies, "Yes, in the arts—because nothing matters but the individual artist."

Much as the man would deny it, H/A is essentially the lengthening shadow of W. McNeil Lowry. He is a rather short man with classically handsome American features masked by the facial lines which make him look considerably older than forty-eight. His walk is a shamble, and his posture wrecks the cut of his blue suits. He speaks with a rather nasal Midwestern drawl. Like most foundation officers, he looks, acts, and reacts like a man who recently had a bad heart attack and has learned to live with his coronary.

Among Lowry's assets are intelligence, efficiency, and a thin-lipped Scotch tightness which reassures his superiors at Ford when they see him walk the halls. He also has considerable native sympathy for the frustration of the arts: he was one of the founders of the ambitious "little" magazine *Accent*, and he has several unperformed plays in a desk drawer at home. His unique value, however, is a startling degree of honesty. Lowry is an honest man, not merely by normal foundation-political-business standards, but by individual ones. People who would not dare to risk such behavior with anyone else will tell Mac Lowry the truth. (One result of this situation is that after people have given Lowry information about themselves, they come back to get information from Lowry about others; H/A is forever advising how things are done elsewhere. As Pryce-Jones puts it, "We run a Universal Aunts bureau"—the reference is to a London baby sitters agency—"as well as a bank.")

"Mac," says Lincoln Kirstein admiringly, "has informed himself as nobody else is informed. He's involved himself in the climate of arts. Mac's interest is an artist's interest, while the interest elsewhere—the interest of the bankers, the lawyers, the real-estate speculators who control the arts—is just ethical. *They* think," Kirstein says with all the scorn of a man who has just quit the Board of Lincoln Center, "*they* think art is something that's good for you."

Nevertheless, Lowry is a foundation man, working for the greatest fund of all. Roscoe Pound once told Abraham Flexner he was not afraid foundations would be radical but that they would be sterile. The Ford Foundation, as a matter of policy, *wants* to be sterile. In the arts it wants to be a eunuch. Questions of style, form, matter, can scarcely be discussed: "Ford," Lowry says, "tries not to influence this situation."

Lowry has no choice. It would be a national scandal if Ford's handful of administrators spent its tax-free money in deliberate efforts to influence artistic style. Yet the situation is not so simple, because anyone with money to spend on the arts must inevitably influence styles. Ultimately the consumer of art decides the survival of styles, and he expresses his taste by the expenditure of money. In effect, the foundation is a consumer. By acting as a consumer without taste, by spreading its largesse equally over declining and rising styles, any neutral supplier of subsidies must over the long run lessen the efficiency of the market and the power of artistic movements.

What called the Ford genie out of the bottle, and threatens to call a Federal arts program to the support of our deficit-crippled artistic institutions, is the decline of the market for art. The situation is confusing, because in absolute terms Americans are spending more than ever on artistic institutions. But there are more Americans and more artists, and the dollar is worth less; and an increasing proportion of the money is going for buildings and curatorial services (including such things as symphony orchestras dedicated to the performance of the Fifty Pieces that constitute the basic repertory from Tokyo to Ashtabula to Cairo). Art originally lived on patronage; then, for a brief period in the nineteenth and twentieth centuries, on the custom of a newly literate, newly sensitized, rapidly growing middle class. Today, the novelty is gone—everyone is literate; the museums are open to all; theater of a sort is available on the same machine that brings you the World Series, Congressional investigations, Presidential elections, and other gladiatorial contests. The artist is no longer the best freak, unless he is the "greatest" artist. A community which regards art as a highly edifying spare-time activity forgets, accidentally or deliberately, that the important form of art is professional art, which can occur only when the professional makes his living at his art. In the absence of funds from the consumers of art, the organizations—businesses, foundations, governments—have been summoned to assume the economic function of the deceased aristocratic patron.

Individual patronage worked, more or less well, centuries ago, because the patron was a consumer: the artist could win his war against the individual patron by charming him, by laying the golden eggs of truth beyond reason, world without end. Foundations and governments do not want such truths and cannot be charmed. If the arts must live on such patronage, they stand condemned to a dead climate of disinterest, to academicism and politics, to hermetic egocentricity. Ultimately H/A can be successful only by putting itself out of business, by raising such a storm of interest in the arts that the audience will once again be willing to pay the costs. Propaganda is no good for this purpose; what is needed is a display of irresistible artistic spectacle.

Not much can be done on three million dollars a year, but Lowry hopes for more. And because he himself can be charmed, because art is important to him not as education but as art, even though he cannot express his tastes, he has been able to make a start toward increasing the visibility of artistic spectacle in America. As an honest man, he cannot say how big a start has been made or how much natural momentum has been developed. "I'm pessimistic on Mondays," says Mac Lowry. "On Tuesdays, I'm optimistic."

Author of Wall Street: Men and Money; Madison Avenue, USA; The Schools, *and of many magazine articles, Martin Mayer is a leading observer of American institutions today.*

In the visual arts one of Ford's largest programs has taken two forms: grants to individual artists, and the financing of retrospective exhibitions of painters and sculptors in mid-career. These shows, first mounted in an artist's home area, circulate around the nation. Carl Morris of Portland and his wife Hilda, opposite, are unique as a couple who have won both forms of aid: abstractionist Morris (see Flowing Arch, *on easel) a show; sculptor Hilda Morris (*Wind Tides, *foreground;* Vaulted Echo, *rear) a $10,000 grant.*

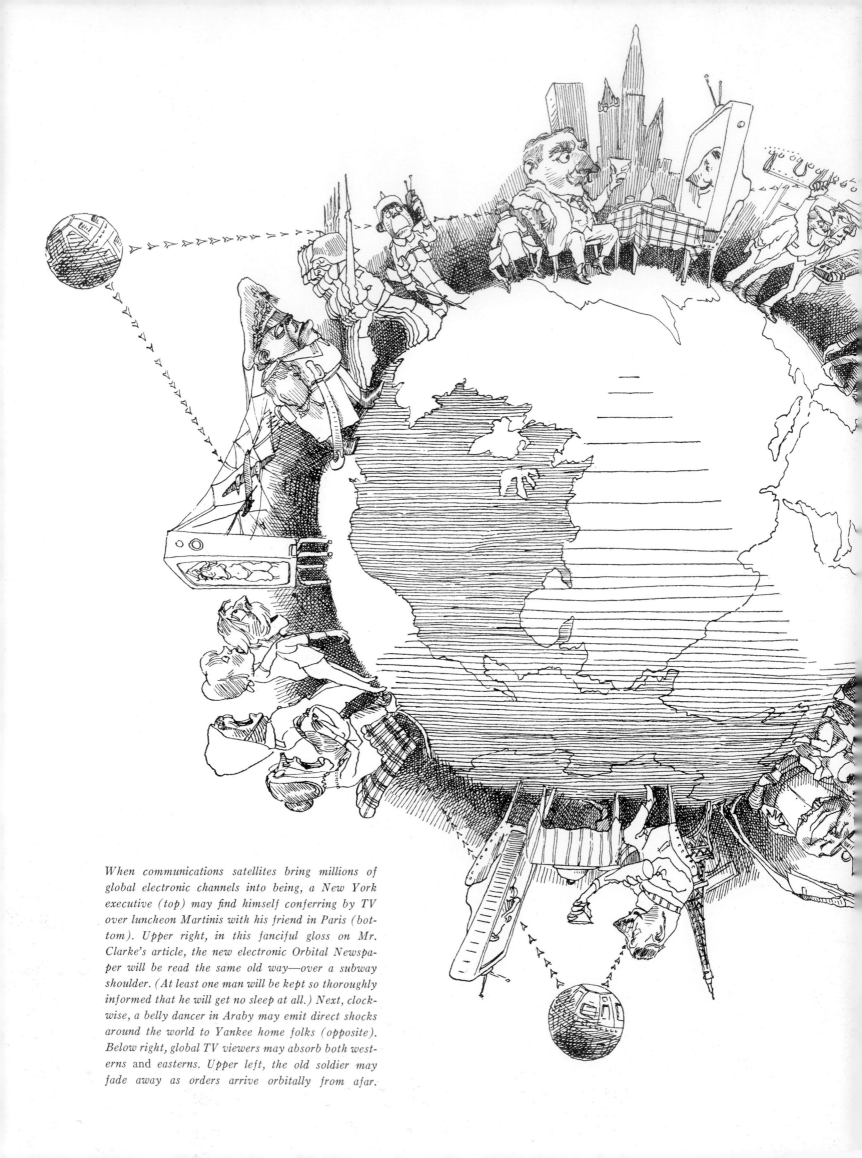

When communications satellites bring millions of global electronic channels into being, a New York executive (top) may find himself conferring by TV over luncheon Martinis with his friend in Paris (bottom). Upper right, in this fanciful gloss on Mr. Clarke's article, the new electronic Orbital Newspaper will be read the same old way—over a subway shoulder. (At least one man will be kept so thoroughly informed that he will get no sleep at all.) Next, clockwise, a belly dancer in Araby may emit direct shocks around the world to Yankee home folks (opposite). Below right, global TV viewers may absorb both westerns and easterns. Upper left, the old soldier may fade away as orders arrive orbitally from afar.

The Social Consequences of the Communications Satellites

The writer who first proposed them foresees:
- *The ten-cent phone call to anywhere*
- *The decline of travel*
- *The death of the printed newspaper*
- *Every library book on your home screen*
- *Instant mail without mailmen*
- *The end of censorship*
- *A universal language (but which one?)*

In the ability to communicate an unlimited range of ideas lies the chief distinction between man and animal; almost everything that is specifically human arises from this power. Society was unthinkable before the invention of speech, civilization impossible before the invention of writing. Half a millennium ago the mechanization of writing by means of the printing press flooded the world with the ideas and knowledge that triggered the Renaissance; little more than a century ago electrical communication began that conquest of distance which has now brought the poles to within a fifteenth of a second of each other. Radio and television have given us a mastery over time and space so miraculous that it seems virtually complete.

Yet it is far from being so; another revolution, perhaps as far-reaching in its effects as printing and electronics, is now upon us. Its agent is the communications satellite.

The suggestion that satellites might be used for relaying radio and TV apparently originated in a technical paper I published in 1945 ["Extra-Terrestrial Relays," in *Wireless World*]; the idea was first realized in December, 1958, when President Eisenhower broadcast his Christmas message to the world by means of a transmitter in an orbiting Atlas missile. Since then, an immense engineering effort has been devoted to communications satellites, and many experimental versions have been launched. Some—like the giant ECHO balloon, which has been seen by millions as a slowly moving star—are merely passive reflectors or radio mirrors, scattering back to Earth a small fraction

By ARTHUR C. CLARKE

of the energy that falls upon them. Others, like COURIER, are active; that is to say, they receive, amplify, and rebroadcast the signals beamed up to them from ground stations. Both types will be used increasingly, until they girdle the world with an invisible cat's cradle of radio and TV circuits.

It is not necessary to go into technicalities to appreciate why such satellites can transform our communications. Until today, the *reliable* range of radio has been limited to a few score of miles, for the simple reason that radio waves—like light—travel in straight lines and so cannot bend round the curve of the Earth. The only thing that makes long-distance radio possible at all is the existence of the ionosphere, that reflecting layer in the upper atmosphere which bounces back the so-called short waves so that they reach the ground again at great distances from the transmitter. In the process they usually acquire considerable distortion and interference; though they may be adequate for speech, they are almost useless for music, as anyone who has listened to a concert on the short-wave bands knows.

For the still shorter waves, which alone can carry television and other sophisticated types of telecommunication service, the situation is even worse. These are not reflected back from the ionosphere at all, but slice straight through it and out into space. They can be used, therefore, only for what is called line-of-sight transmissions; you cannot (except under freak conditions) pick up a television station from much farther away than you could see it in perfectly clear air. This is why television transmitters, and the microwave relays now used to carry hundreds of simultaneous telephone circuits across the country, are all sited on towers or mountains to obtain maximum range.

Satellites allow the communications engineer to place his equipment, in effect, on the top of a tower hundreds or even thousands of miles high. A single satellite-borne transmitter could broadcast to almost half the Earth, instead of to an area fifty miles in radius; three of them, spaced equally round the equator, could provide any type of communication service between any two points on the globe. This is something that has never before been possible, and it is going to happen within the next few years, for every major firm in the electronics business is now preparing to get into orbit. This is the great Gold Rush of the 1960's, for on the ultrashort radio—and even light—waves which the satellites can flash around the world there is room for millions of television and *billions* of telephone channels.

What effect will the new types of communications services, and the vastly increased numbers of existing ones, have upon our society and our culture? Before we attempt to answer that, it is worth remembering that it is never possible to foresee the full impact of a major invention, or even of a minor one. Look, for example, at the effect of the humble typewriter, which liberated one half of the human race from centuries of subservience. We males have conveniently forgotten just how few were the occupations—and fewer still the respectable ones—open to women a lifetime ago. Mr. Remington changed all that, and the revolution he wrought was trifling compared with that produced by Henry Ford a little later with the Model T.

Yet communication affects us even more vitally and directly than transportation. A man can live a full and rich life without ever stirring from one spot, so long as he has sufficient channels of information. It is only our age that has made a fetish of rushing around the world; if I remember correctly, it was Aldous Huxley who remarked that speed is the only new vice invented by modern man. Communications satellites, though they may themselves be moving at fifteen thousand miles an hour, may have a remarkably stabilizing influence on the human race. They will abolish a vast amount of the traveling and even of the day-to-day commuting that now seems an unavoidable part of our lives.

For communications satellites will enable us, in effect, to move almost instantaneously to any part of the world. A few figures should be enough to demonstrate this point.

The oceans have always been a major barrier to communications. It required a gigantic effort of technology to provide a telephone cable between Europe and America, carrying only thirty-six voice circuits at a cost of more than a million dollars *each*. Later cables can carry about a hundred circuits, but there is not much room for further improvement—and it would take ten cables, costing perhaps a quarter of a billion dollars, to provide a single television circuit.

Yet a fairly modest satellite, which we can build today, could provide a thousand voice channels across the Atlantic, or alternatively a single television circuit. Looking only a decade or two into the future, one can foresee the time when a network of advanced satellites will bring all points on the Earth into close contact so far as telephony is concerned. It will be as quick and easy to call Australia from Greenland, or South America from China, as it is now to put through a local call. Indeed, by the end of this century *all* terrestrial calls may be local calls and may be billed at a flat standard rate.

This may have as great an effect on business and social life as the invention of the telephone itself. Just how great that was, we of today have forgotten; perhaps we can remind ourselves by imagining that the telephone was suddenly abolished and we had to conduct all business face to face or else by correspondence carried by stagecoach and sailing ship. To our grandchildren we will still seem in that primitive level of development, and our present patterns of daily commuting a fantastic nightmare. For ask yourself how much traveling you would *really* have to do if you had an office in your own home equipped with a few simple information-handling machines and wide-screen, full-color television through which you could be in face-to-face contact with anyone on Earth. A good nine tenths of the traveling that now takes place could be avoided with better communications.

There can be no doubt that satellites will have an especially great effect on the transmission of written and printed information. One idea that has been discussed at some length is the Orbital Post Office, which may make most air mail obsolete in a decade or so. A single satellite, using modern facsimile equipment, could easily handle the whole of today's transatlantic correspondence. Eventually, letters should never take more than a few minutes to be delivered to any point on the Earth, and one can even visualize the time when all correspondence is sent by direct person-to-person facsimile circuits. When that time comes, the post office will cease to handle letters, except where the originals are required, and will concern itself only with parcels.

Another development that will have the most far-reaching consequences is the Orbital Newspaper; this is inevitable once the idea gets around that what most people need is information, not wood pulp. Half a century from now, newspapers as we know them may not exist, except as trains of electronic impulses. When you wish to read the New York *Times*, you will dial the appropriate number on your channel selector, just as today you call a party on the telephone. The front page would then appear on your high-definition screen, at least as sharp and clear as on a microfilm reader; it would remain there until you pressed a button, when it would be replaced by page two, and so on.

Of course, the entire format would be completely redesigned for the new medium; perhaps there would be separate channels for editorials, book reviews, business, news, classified advertising, etc. If you needed a permanent record (and just how often *do* you save your daily paper?), that could easily be arranged by an attachment like a Polaroid camera or one of the high-speed copying devices now found in all modern offices.

Not only the local paper but all the papers of all countries could be viewed in this way, merely by dialing the right number—and back issues, too, since this would require nothing more than appropriate extra coding.

This leads us directly into the enormous and exciting field of information storage and retrieval, which is one of the basic problems of our culture. It is now possible to store any written material or any illustration in electronic form—as, for example, is done every day on video tape. One can thus envisage a Central Library, or Memory Bank, which would be a permanent part of the world communications network. Readers and scholars could call for any document, from the Declaration of Independence to the current best seller, and see it flashed on their screens.

The Electronic Library is bound to come, its development being forced by the rising flood of printed matter. Recently, a storage device was announced that could contain everything ever written or printed on stone, paper, or papyrus during the last ten thousand years inside a six-foot cube. The problem of encoding and indexing all the world's literature in electronic form so that any part of it can be retrieved and played back is a staggering one, but it has to be solved before our libraries collapse under the weight of their books. And when it is solved, any man on Earth who knows how to dial the right numbers will have immediate access to all printed knowledge, flashed from Central Memory Bank up to the nearest satellite and down again to be displayed on the screen of his receiver. If he wishes, he will be able to store it in his own electronic library for easy reference, as we now record music or conversation on tape—although the recording medium will certainly be much more compact and convenient.

The most glamourous possibility opened up by communications satellites is the one which I originally stressed in 1945—global radio and television. This will be something quite new in the world, and we have no precedents to guide us. For the first time one nation will be able to speak directly to the people of another, and to project images into their homes—with or without the co-operation of the other government concerned. Today's short-wave sound broadcasts are only poor and feeble things compared to those which the clear, interference-free reception from satellites will make possible.

I sometimes wonder if the enormous efforts that most large nations now expend on short-wave broadcasting are worth it, in view of the poor quality of reception. But this will change when the direct and far more efficient line-of-sight services from satellites become available; a Londoner, for example, will be able to tune into NBC or CBS or Radio Moscow as easily and clearly as to the BBC. The engineers and scientists now struggling to establish reliable satellite circuits with the aid of antennas the size of football fields will tell you that this is still years in the future, and they may be right. Nevertheless, most of us will see the day when every home will be fitted with radio and TV equipment that can tune directly to transmitters orbiting thousands of miles above the Earth, and the last barriers to free communications will be down.

Those who are already glutted with entertainment and information from their local stations may be less than enthusiastic about this. However, they are a tiny minority of the human race. Most of the world does not even have radio, still less television. I would suggest, therefore, that though the first use of satellites will be to provide increased facilities between already highly developed countries, their greatest political and cultural influence will be upon backward and even preliterate peoples.

For in the 1970's we will be able to put megawatt transmitters into orbit and will also have reliable battery-powered television receivers that can be mass-produced at a cost which even small African or Asian villages can afford.

Quite apart from its direct visual impact, the effect of TV will be incomparably greater than that of radio because it is so much less dependent upon language. Men can enjoy pictures even when they cannot understand the words that go with them. Moreover, the pictures may encourage them to understand those words. If it is used properly, global television could be the greatest force yet discovered for breaking down the linguistic barriers that prevent communication between men.

Nobody knows how many languages there are in the world; estimates run to as high as six thousand. But a mere seven are spoken by half the human race, and it is interesting to list the percentages. First by a substantial margin comes Mandarin, the language of 15 per cent of mankind. Then comes English, 10 per cent. After that there is a large gap, and grouped together round the 5 per cent level we find in this order: Hindustani, Spanish, Russian, German, and Japanese. But these are *mother* tongues, and far more people understand English than normally speak it. On the basis of world comprehension, English undoubtedly leads all other languages.

Few subjects touch upon national pride and prejudices as much as does language, yet everyone recognizes the immense value and importance of a tongue which all educated men can understand. I think that, within a lifetime, communications satellites may give us just that. Unless some synthetic language comes to the fore—which seems improbable—the choice appears to be between Mandarin, English, and, for obvious reasons, Russian—even though it is only fifth on the list and understood by less than 5 per cent of mankind. Perhaps it will be a photo finish, and our grandchildren will be bi- or trilingual. I will venture no predictions, but I would stress again that it is impossible to underestimate the importance of communications satellites in this particular domain.

Television satellites will also present us, and that, soon, with acute problems in international relations. Suppose country A starts transmitting what the government of country B considers to be subversive propaganda. This is happening all the time, of course, but no one complains too bitterly today because the process is relatively ineffective and is confined to radio. Just imagine, however, what Dr. Goebbels could have done with a chain of global TV stations, perhaps capable of putting down stronger signals in many countries than could be produced by the local transmitters—if any.

There would be only two ways of countering such unwanted propaganda. An aggrieved government might try to prevent the sale of receivers that could tune to the offending frequencies, or it might try jamming. Neither policy would be very effective, and jamming could only be carried out from another satellite—which would probably cause protests from the rest of the world, owing to the interference with legitimate transmissions elsewhere.

Though there are obvious dangers and possibilities of friction, on the whole I am very optimistic about this breaking down of national communications barriers, holding to the old-fashioned belief that in the long run right will prevail. I also look forward, with more than a little interest, to the impact of non-commercial television upon audiences which so far have not had much choice in the matter. Millions of Americans have never known the joys of sponsorless radio or television; they are like readers who know only books full of advertisements *which they are not allowed to skip*. How would reading have fared, in these circumstances? And how will Madison Avenue fare, when it no longer controls the video channels? Perhaps the apocalypse of the agencies has already been described in Revelation, chapter 18: ". . . And the merchants of the earth shall weep and mourn . . . for no man buyeth their merchandise any more: The merchandise of gold, and silver, and precious stones . . . and ointments . . . and wine, and oil . . . and chariots . . . and souls of men." This last commodity, I believe, is one expended in massive quantities by commercial television.

The old problem of censorship, over which the law and literature have so often come to grips in dubious battle, will certainly be aggravated when all forms of censorship become impossible. The Postmaster General, that traditional guardian of morals, will have no effective control over the ether—nor will anyone else. The possibilities of really uninhibited telecasting from space, if any country was unscrupulous enough to defy normal conventions for the sake of attracting viewers to its channels, are somewhat hairraising. The crime, bloodshed, and violence for which TV has been so heavily criticized, and the unspeakable "horror comics" that have flooded the Western world in so many millions since the war, show what can happen even in societies that consider themselves enlightened. There will always be people who, to sell their wares or their policies, are willing to appeal to the lowest instincts. They may one day be able to do this across all borders, without hindrance.

But the ether is morally as neutral as the printed page, and on the whole, censorship does more harm than good.

Communications satellites can bring to every home on Earth sadism and pornography, vapid parlor games or inflated egos, all-in wrestling or tub-thumping revivalism. Yet they can also expose lies and spread the truth; no dictatorship can build a wall high enough to stop its citizens' listening to the voices from the stars.

These are some of the obvious and predictable effects of communications satellites, but there will be others much more subtle that will have even more profound effects upon the structure of our society. Consider the automobile once again; when it was invented, the assertion was made that it would be useful only in cities—because here alone were there roads on which it could operate. Well, in our efforts to free the automobile from an urban existence, we changed the face of the world and abolished immemorial ways of life. With that analogy in mind, I would like to suggest that the communications satellite may have as great an effect upon *time* as the automobile has had upon *space*.

The fact that the world is round and it is thus noon in Washington when it is midnight in Mandalay inconvenienced nobody in the leisurely days before the airplane and the radio. It is different now: most of us have had to take overseas phone calls in the middle of the night or have had our eating and sleeping schedules disrupted by jet transport from one time zone to another. What is inconvenient today will be quite intolerable in ten or twenty years as our communications networks extend to cover the globe. Can you imagine the situation if in your own town a third of your friends and acquaintances were asleep whenever you wanted to contact them? Yet this is a close parallel to what will happen in a world of cheap and instantaneous communications—*unless we change the patterns of our lives*.

We cannot abolish time zones, unless we beat the Earth into a flat disc like an LP record. But I suggest, in all seriousness, that the advent of global telephony and television will lead to a major attack on the problem of sleep. It has been obvious for a long time that we can't afford to spend twenty years of our lives in unconsciousness, and many people have already stopped doing so. You can now buy in the USSR a little five-pound box that keeps you in such deep slumber, through electronic pulses applied to the temples, that you require only one or two hours of sleep per day.

This suggestion may seem to be fantasy; I believe it barely hints at some of the changes that communications satellites will bring about. What we are building now is the nervous system of mankind, which will link together the whole human race, for better or worse, in a unity which no earlier age could have imagined. The communications network, of which the satellites will be nodal points, will enable the consciousness of our grandchildren to flicker like lightning back and forth across the face of this planet. They will be able to go anywhere and meet anyone, at any time, without stirring from their homes. All knowledge will be open to them, all the museums and libraries of the world will be extensions of their living rooms. Marvelous machines, with unlimited information-handling capacity, will be able to speak directly into their minds.

And there's the rub, for the machines can far outpace the capacities of their builders. Already, we are punch-drunk with the news, information, and entertainment that bombard us from a thousand sources. How can we possibly cope with the far greater flood to come, when the whole world —soon, indeed, the whole solar system—will be clamoring for our attention?

There is a Persian legend that warns us of what may come from our efforts to devise a communications system linking all mankind. The story tells of a prince who lost his dearly loved queen and devoted the rest of his life to building a monument that would be worthy of her. He hired the finest craftsmen to raise a palace of marble and alabaster around the sarcophagus; year by year it grew until its towers and minarets became the wonder of the world. Decade after decade he labored, but still perfection eluded him; there was some fundamental flaw in the design.

And then one day, as the prince stood on the gallery above the central aisle of the great mausoleum, he realized what it was that spoiled the perfect harmony. He called the architect and pointed to the now dwarfed sarcophagus that held the queen he had lost so long ago.

"Take that thing away," he said.

So it may be with us. The communications network we are building may be such a technological masterpiece, such a miracle of power and speed and complexity, that it will have no place for man's slow and limited brain. In the end there will be a time when only machines can talk to machines, and we must tiptoe away and leave them to it.

This is an adaptation of a lecture given by Mr. Clarke, the noted British science writer, space student, and novelist, before the XIIth International Astronautical Congress.

DRAWINGS BY DAVID LEVINE

THE
VATICAN

BENEATH ITS RENAISSANCE PALACES AND BAROQUE

BASILICA LIES THE EARTH OF PAGAN ROME, FOR

HERE THE ACCUMULATED SPLENDOR OF CENTURIES

UNITES THE TWIN SOURCES OF OUR CIVILIZATION:

CLASSICAL ANTIQUITY AND THE CHRISTIAN CHURCH

By ALFRED WERNER

Opposite: This is the interior of Old St. Peter's as it looked in the sixteenth century, shortly before it was torn down to make way for the great Renaissance and baroque church that today rises so much more grandly in its place. Constantine the Great built it in the fourth century A.D. *above the presumed grave of the Apostle Peter, and there it stood for more than a thousand years—often altered, restored, and refurbished, but still essentially the same. This anonymous fresco was probably painted during the demolition, as a record of what was about to vanish forever. The bronze pine cone in the foreground, perhaps some relic of an ancient Roman bath, did not actually stand in the church itself but in the atrium. It is still part of the Vatican treasure and may be seen in the palace courtyard (see page 48). Along with a few fragments and foundation stones, it is all that survives of what was for so long the most venerated church in Christendom.*

"The beauty of the Piazza in which it stands, with its clusters of exquisite columns and its gushing fountains—so fresh, so broad, and free and beautiful—nothing can exaggerate. The first burst of the interior, in all its expansive majesty and glory, and most of all, the looking up into the Dome, is a sensation never to be forgotten."

Thus wrote the dazzled young Charles Dickens almost one hundred and twenty years ago. Before him and after him, men of letters have written tributes to St. Peter's, as well as to the Sistine Chapel, to the Laocoön group, and to the other treasures of the Vatican, yet they take for granted the presence of all these splendid buildings and artifacts in what is now known as the Stato della Città del Vaticano. Indeed, it is difficult to imagine a time when it all did not exist, or when the more than one hundred acres of papal territory harbored less than the astonishing accretion of significant edifices and luxurious gardens that today delights the traveler. Like the Taj Mahal, the Louvre, the Acropolis, or the Pyramids, this vast complex of buildings and trees west of the Tiber, inside the boundaries of the city of Rome yet a sovereign and independent entity, seems to be as timeless, as old, as the very foundations of Rome. But it is not all that old: when Dickens crossed the Tiber in 1844, the sight that provoked his hymn to architectural beauty had received its final shape less than two hundred years before. The magnificent dome of St. Peter's rising 452 feet to the top of the golden cross, the massive pillars of the colonnades, outstretched like arms to embrace the visitor, were completed only in the seventeenth century. Precious few of the buildings on Vatican hill are older than the fifteenth century.

The Church was anything but hospitable to artists and architects in the beginning. In its earliest days, when the Church was not only poor but was considered "subversive," places of worship were by necessity small and unimpressive. Even after Christianity's victory over its rivals, there were many of its leaders who expressed doubts as to the propriety of venerating images and who opposed all ostentation. Yet while the early Christians were despised by the pagan world for their lack of altars, temples, images, or tangible representations of God, far-seeing churchmen as early as the fourth century began to enlist the fine arts in the service of Christianity. And the sixth-century pope, Gregory the Great, dismayed at the destruction of sacred pictures in one of his dioceses, issued this warning to all iconoclasts: "It is one thing to worship a picture and another to learn from the image of a picture what this is which ought to be worshiped. What those who can read learn by means of writing, that do the uneducated learn by looking at a picture."

For this pontiff, art existed "solely for instructing the minds of the ignorant," but some of the Renaissance popes, like some of the Roman emperors, were connoisseurs in the modern sense who could derive deep aesthetic pleasure from a fine painting or an excellent piece of sculpture, whether the subject was religious or secular. In the Middle Ages many a voice was raised against building huge, richly adorned and expensive churches in the service of a religion that had been founded by humble craftsmen and fishermen. Thus in the twelfth century Saint Bernard of Clairvaux severely rebuked the Order of Cluniac Benedictines for "the vast height of your churches, their immoderate length, their

Michelangelo's last job at the Vatican was to design a dome for the new St. Peter's. The painting opposite shows him pointing out the details of a scale model to Pope Paul IV, but he died before he could execute it. The result is somewhat different from what he intended. In fact, the final version of St. Peter's (seen here from the rear, with the piazza beyond and the papal palaces at middle left) probably would not please any of its several architects, but for sheer monumentality it has no match. Any of the world's great cathedrals could fit comfortably inside it (diagram at right).

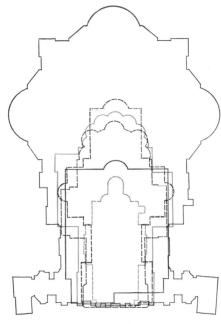

St. Peter's
St. Paul's
Cologne
Chartres
Hagia Sophia
St. Patrick's

Bramante's design, c. 1506

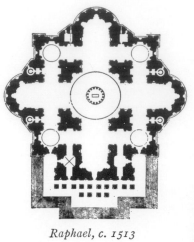

Raphael, c. 1513

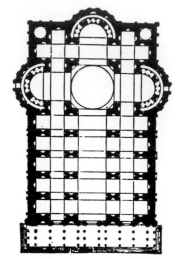

Michelangelo, c. 1546

superfluous breadth, the costly polishings, the curious carvings and paintings which attract the worshiper's gaze and hinder his attention."

Had Saint Bernard's views prevailed, none of the great churches of England, France, Germany, Italy, and Spain would have been built, and Giotto, Fra Angelico, Michelangelo, and Raphael might never have flourished. But luckily for mankind, many of the popes were patrons who commissioned new works of art from painters and sculptors and eagerly acquired others from all ages and regions of the world. And even though it is known that the headstrong Pope Julius II on occasion tried to browbeat Michelangelo, and even though Veronese had difficulties with the Inquisition for interpreting religious dogma in too secular and realistic a manner, as a rule the Church did not interfere with an artist's own vision.

Walking through St. Peter's, and through those rooms that have been opened to the public in the gigantic maze to the north, one can easily imagine himself in a period when the Roman Catholic Church, though challenged by the new forces of Martin Luther, was the most powerful institution in the world. But it is more difficult to envisage the first one thousand years of St. Peter's and the Vatican. Since 1939, excavations have revealed a veritable necropolis under St. Peter's, a labyrinth of Roman and early Christian sepulchres with mosaics and vaulted arches. Pilgrims continue to kneel in the sunken area called the *Confessio*, reputed to be the burial place of the Apostle Peter; but archaeologists have not found his grave or any bones that indubitably could be considered his. All that can be said is that Constantine the Great built his church where the martyred saint was believed to have been buried.

Though archaeological evidence is lacking, Saint Peter may very well have been executed as an enemy of the Roman state on or near Vatican hill, and he may very well have been buried in the pagan cemetery that lies beneath St. Peter's and is now in part accessible to visitors. On the same spot a small shrine seems to have already existed before the Emperor Constantine began the erection of a large basilica sometime between A.D. 307 and 337. (He is said to have participated in the work with his own hands, himself carrying twelve baskets of earth in honor of the Twelve Apostles.) By the year 800, when Pope Leo III crowned Charlemagne Emperor of the West there, the church—enlarged from its humble beginnings—must have looked very majestic and impressive for its time. But Old St. Peter's was made of brick and wood and covered barely half the area occupied by the present church; it was a simple basilican hall with transepts and a single apse, and very little of it survives. Perhaps the only relic of Old St. Peter's the traveler will notice is a late adornment, the large bronze doors commissioned by Pope Eugenius IV from Filarete, a quattrocento sculptor. There, in relief, are a variety of scenes depicting mythological and historical events, some glorifying the pontificate of the artist's patron. Completed in 1445, the doors were incorporated in the new basilica in 1620 and still shield its central entrance.

The origins of the Vatican are also shrouded in darkness. Does the name itself come from a vanished Etruscan town, or from the Latin word *vaticinii*, meaning oracles or prophe-

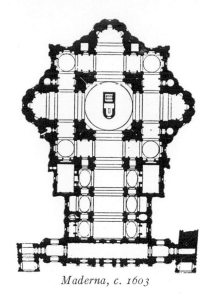

Maderna, c. 1603

Crowds that flocked to the coronation of Pope Sixtus V in 1585 could see the new dome rising (but slowly: it had looked that way for twenty years) directly behind the crumbling façade of Old St. Peter's. The series of floor plans shows how the new basilica evolved from Bramante's scheme (far left) through Raphael's and Michelangelo's to, finally, that of Maderna (above).

cies? The first papal residence on Vatican hill, a sparsely inhabited section on the Tiber's right bank, was erected by Pope Symmachus around the year 500 near the forecourt of Old St. Peter's. It was rebuilt and enlarged in the twelfth and thirteenth centuries (unfortunately, no description of this early compound, nor any graphic record of it, survives). But the home of the popes during the Middle Ages was the Lateran Palace across the river, and the Vatican was used only on state occasions and for the reception of foreign sovereigns visiting Rome. During most of the fourteenth century—that is to say, throughout their "Babylonian captivity"—the popes dwelt in Avignon in southern France; and it was only after 1377, when Gregory XI brought the papacy back to Rome, that the Lateran, completely dilapidated and unfit for dwelling, was abandoned for the Vatican.

Some of the fifteenth-century popes may have felt that the combination of living quarters, offices, and archives to the north of St. Peter's was comfortable and adequate, but this feeling was not shared by Cardinal Parentucelli, who in 1447 ascended the papal throne as Nicholas V. He was the first in the remarkable series of Renaissance popes, and was one of the foremost Christian humanists of his time. This great admirer of classical Greek literature assembled a large library of books superbly bound and stamped with his own coat of arms. So considerable was his erudition that a colleague, Aeneas Silvius (later to become Pius II), said of him: "What he does not know is outside the range of human knowledge." Since Old St. Peter's, after a thousand years, was falling into ruin, and the Vatican, in his eyes, was not a sight the Church could be proud of, Nicholas drew up, with

the help of the celebrated Florentine architect Leon Battista Alberti, ambitious plans for the reconstruction of both.

The famous nineteenth-century German historian Gregorovius said, "The man who was capable of conceiving such a work of art as St. Peter's and of beginning to execute it, deserves, by that fact alone, to live forever in the memory of mankind." Was Alberti that man? It is true that he envisaged St. Peter's very much, in general outline, the way it was to look two hundred years later (including Bernini's colonnade), but Nicholas died before Alberti's vision could be developed beyond the sketch pad. Nor was Nicholas V himself exactly the man Gregorovius described, although he still merits first place in the long line of "building popes" admired by posterity for the magnitude of their architectural schemes yet severely criticized by their own contemporaries for their prodigality with funds.

Still, whatever charges might have been lodged against some of Nicholas's successors, he himself was an extraordinary man. Death prevented him from carrying out his plans for rebuilding St. Peter's (he started to raze the apse of Constantine's old basilica, but that was as far as he got). His real monument is the Vatican Library, which he founded. Nicholas sent his agents to the far ends of the world to gather manuscripts and books for the Library which today has more than half a million volumes, seven thousand incunabula, and sixty thousand manuscripts, including some of the rarest and most ancient—among them the *Codex Vaticanus,* one of two fourth-century versions of the Bible in Greek. His other monument is the now-famous Chapel of Nicholas V, which he had decorated with scenes drawn from

TEXT CONTINUED ON PAGE 31

As old as St. Peter's, is the tradition that it was built over the grave of the Apostle himself, but no one knew what really lay beneath the church until 1939. In that year Vatican workmen started lowering the floor of the crypt and ran into Roman masonry. Pope Pius XII ordered a full investigation, and the first thing to be excavated was this handsome mausoleum built by the family of the Cae-tennii in the second century A.D. Since then the diggers have found a whole Roman cemetery and the ancient shrine of Saint Peter, above which Constantine built his basilica—but nothing that can be positively identified as the martyred Apostle's grave.

IAM TANDEM
CHRISTVM
LIBERE PRO
FITERI LICET

This painting by Giulio Romano commemorates a historic event that never actually took place: Constantine's granting of political dominion over Rome, Italy, and the West to the papacy. It shows the Emperor kneeling before Pope Sylvester, his gift of temporal power symbolized by a golden statuette. Even before this was painted about 1520, the document embodying Constantine's "Donation" had come under suspicion, and the Church has long since declared it a forgery. The fresco provides another view of Old St. Peter's, different from the one on page 22 in that it includes a screen of twisted columns between the nave and the altar, which was built above the ancient shrine of Saint Peter.

TEXT CONTINUED FROM PAGE 27

the lives of Saints Stephen and Lawrence. These works reveal a mastery of style midway between Gothic fervor and Renaissance freedom, and a single-minded piety that earned the artist Fra Giovanni da Fiesole the appropriate name "Angelico." These frescoes, with their lavish use of gold, light, and brilliant colors, highly stylized and yet the most direct spiritual expression of a most unworldly man, were forgotten for a long time. The room at one point had been bricked up and was not rediscovered until an architect began to investigate an unaccounted-for space in the palace's plans.

Credit for having opened the Vatican Library to public use goes, however, to Sixtus IV (1471–1484). This pope was perhaps not a wholly admirable figure. Nepotism was rampant during his reign, and his nominations to the cardinalate were often far from wise. Yet he was a great patron of the arts: he bestowed his name on the Sistine Choir, which he founded, and he built both the Sistine Bridge across the Tiber and the world's most famous shrine of art, the Sistine Chapel.

In the mid-twentieth century we are inclined to believe that Nicholas V should not have started razing Old St. Peter's and should have planned to build whatever church he had in mind on some other site, perhaps next to Constantine's edifice, respecting the age and aesthetic significance of the early basilica. Similarly, we cannot help feeling uneasy about the highhanded manner in which the Sistine Chapel, as originally built in the 1470's, was dealt with in the following century. To make room for the expansive genius of Michelangelo, several frescoes by Perugino were washed off one of the side walls. (It was then customary to treat works of art with less respect than nowadays, and frescoes were changed with the casualness that walls are repainted today for each new tenant. Julius II had all the frescoes removed when he moved into new living quarters in the Vatican Palace.) In any event, when Sixtus IV died in 1484, his chapel was not the overwhelming place it is today, for it still lacked the major contributions by Michelangelo, who was then only a boy of nine.

Though Sixtus IV was hardly the ideal pope, Innocent VIII, who followed him, was so corrupt that he aroused the violent anger of the Dominican friar Girolamo Savonarola. Innocent's only contribution to the Vatican was the building of a summer home, the Villa Belvedere. While the interior decorations done by Mantegna have perished, Vasari has preserved in his *Lives of the Artists* an anecdote revealing that the Prince of the Church was as lax in his financial obligations toward his artists as he was gifted with a sense of humor: "Who is she?" Innocent asked, finding Mantegna at work on a figure whose meaning he could not guess. "Economy, your Holiness," the artist replied emphatically. "Paint next to her Patience, Mantegna," the Pope advised, but from that day on never delayed the artist's pay.

The more secular the Church became, the more did the Vatican grow in artistic splendor. Those popes who were the

31

least religious, least spiritual, among the more than two hundred and fifty successors to Saint Peter, were also those who contributed the most toward embellishing the Holy See with first-rate works of art. Innocent VIII may not correspond to our notion of all that a pontiff should be, but it is even more difficult to view Rodrigo Borgia as the supreme head of the Roman Catholic Church and the shepherd of all Christians. There is no doubt that he was responsible for some of the crimes attributed to him, yet much of what was said and written against him was slander. That he had above all the aggrandizement of his immediate family in mind is probably true, but the stories of orgies and the strangling of his kidnapped enemies in the so-called Borgia apartments of the Vatican are open to doubt. For he is also known to us as a brilliant man who loved music and the theater and enjoyed the company of savants; as cardinal he wrote several theological treatises, and as Pope Alexander VI he revitalized the University of Rome.

While he added to the Vatican only the tower that to this day is called Torre Borgia, the decoration of the apartments that carry the family's name is his real contribution. To provide frescoes for the six rooms he called upon Pinturic-

chio, a deaf, decrepit little painter of unusual talent. Between 1492 and 1495 Pinturicchio and his assistants covered the walls with some of the world's loveliest pageants, combining legends of early Christianity with the twilit mystery of the Umbrian landscape and the fantasy of the Orient.

Pope Julius II (1503–1513) despised his Borgia predecessor so much that he refused to inhabit the apartment polluted by Alexander VI and his court and chose to live on the floor above. Unlike Alexander, who was a shrewd and ruthless politician, Julius II, *"Il terribile,"* of indomitable will, was primarily a soldier fighting for the greater glory of his Church. But he was also one of the greatest art patrons the Roman Catholic Church has ever had, and it was he who actually started rebuilding St. Peter's. The architect Bramante, who had already worked for Alexander VI, under Julius came to occupy something like the position of minister of public works and fine arts at the Papal Court—accompanying Julius on all journeys, planning all fortifications, and rebuilding the Vatican as well as St. Peter's. Julius wanted the new St. Peter's to surpass all other churches in the world in its proportions and its splendor and, with his preference for the colossal, approved heartily of Bramante's

TEXT CONTINUED ON PAGE 41

THE TREASURES OF THE VATICAN

A Portfolio from a new Skira book

A year ago Horizon asked the famous Swiss art publisher Albert Skira to prepare a book on the vast variety and richness of the art treasures of St. Peter's and the Vatican museums. The following eight pages present a portfolio selected from the plates in the book, which will be published next month in several languages.

The cross on the facing page, made in Italy about A.D. 600, was left to the Church by Pope Paschal I and buried beneath an altar in the chapel of the Lateran Palace, where it remained until 1903. Its scenes depict: top, the Annunciation and the Visitation; left arm, the Flight into Egypt; center, the Nativity; right arm, the Adoration of the Magi; bottom, the Circumcision and the Baptism of Jesus.

The two following plates show other early treasures. The mosaic depicts Pope John VII wearing the square halo of a living benefactor of the Church and holding symbolically the chapel to Saint Mary which he built in Constantine's basilica. Originally placed in the chapel, the mosaic was later moved to the grottoes of St. Peter's, where it was only discovered in the recent excavations. The altarpiece which faces it bears the signature of "Giovanni and Niccolò," two painters of the eleventh-century Benedictine School who are otherwise lost to history.

The Belvedere Torso, so called because it is in what used to be the Vatican's Villa Belvedere, is the work of a Greek sculptor, Apollonius, who worked in Rome in the first century B.C. Probably copied from an earlier Greek original, it may represent Her-

cules or Polyphemus. Its influence is clearly visible in the sculpture and painting of Michelangelo, who called himself "a pupil of the Torso." His Libyan Sibyl is one of the five legendary Roman prophetesses whom he painted on the walls of the Sistine Chapel to symbolize pre-Christian perception of the Word of God.

The sixth plate is a portrait of the Borgia pope, Alexander VI. Pinturicchio painted his worldly patron into his fresco of *The Resurrection.*

The seventh plate is a detail from Botticelli's fresco in the Sistine Chapel representing *Scenes from the Life of Moses.* The youth and the old man, dressed in High Renaissance fashion, are supposed to be Israelites in the Exodus.

The last plate, by Fra Angelico, depicts a saint and martyr of the third century. Ordered by the Romans to deliver the possessions of the Church, Saint Lawrence assembled the poor, gave them everything of value, and then told the Roman prefect that the poor were the Church's treasure. For this he was roasted alive.

These plates, as well as the book from which they have been taken, were engraved and printed in Geneva by the slow, painstaking, fine-screen process for which Skira art books are renowned. *The Treasures of the Vatican* contains 85 color plates as well as many black and white reproductions, all individually tipped onto the pages as in this portfolio. The text is by the Italian art expert Maurizio Calvesi, with an introduction by Dr. Deoclecio Redig de Campos, Curator of the Vatican museums.

Gold and enamel cross, components from sixth to ninth centuries. Museo Sacro

Pope John VII, eighth century mosaic, Vatican Grottoes

The Last Judgment by Giovanni and Niccolò, eleventh century altarpiece, Vatican Picture Gallery

Belvedere Torso, Greco-Roman, first century B.C., Vatican Museum

The Libyan Sibyl by Michelangelo, Sistine Ceiling, 1508-1512

Portrait of Pope Alexander VI from *The Resurrection* by Pinturicchio, Borgia Apartments, 1492-1495

Detail of the Exodus from *Scenes from the Life of Moses* by Botticelli, Sistine Chapel, 1481-1482

St. Lawrence Distributing Alms by Fra Angelico, Chapel of Nicholas V, 1447-1455

plan to build a commanding central dome resting on a Greek cross, with four small domes on the four arms. On April 18, 1506, the Pope, accompanied by cardinals and prelates, went to the excavation site to bless the white marble foundation stone bearing an inscription to the effect that he, Julius II, had engaged on this task to restore a basilica which had fallen into decay. He did not live to see the building's completion. Twelve decades were to pass before the last bit of work on it was finished.

To build the new St. Peter's, Julius asked for money from bishops all over Europe. He spent more than seventy thousand gold ducats on it. It is not known how much, in the course of years, Julius spent on Michelangelo and Raphael, the two artists whose names he was fortunate enough to link forever with his own, but we do know that he was penurious and that he was unreasonably impatient. Michelangelo got a commission that would be any artist's dream: to cover the ten-thousand-square-foot ceiling of the Sistine Chapel with scenes from the Old Testament. But in an argument about the speed of the work the Pope struck him with his staff and threatened to have him thrown from the scaffolding.

Michelangelo worked "with great inconvenience to himself, having to labor with his face turned upward." According to Vasari, he "impaired his eyesight so much in the process of the work that he could neither read letters nor examine drawings for several months afterward, except in the same attitude of looking upward." In his own letters the artist complained: "I am more exhausted than man ever was. . . . I live here in great distress and the utmost bodily fatigue, have no friends and seek none. I have not even time enough to eat what I require."

Though one may envisage Michelangelo as an aging, dissatisfied man, he was actually only thirty-seven when the ceiling paintings were finished, and unlike his patron, who died a few months later, he had yet more than half a century to live. Julius, while pleased that his dream had come true, was not entirely satisfied with the work. He objected to the muted color scheme, and thought Michelangelo might still improve his work by touching it up with lustrous colors, particularly gold. This time the artist was adamant, saying that the prophets and holy men, while they were rich in spiritual wealth, were not so in material goods.

Michelangelo already had some major works to his credit, including the statue of David, when he started working for Julius. Raphael, however, was only a lad of twenty-five, without experience in large-scale work, when the Pope chose him from a corps of artists to decorate several rooms. His frescoes in the Vatican Stanze, particularly the *Disputà*, the *School of Athens*, and the *Parnassus* in the Stanza della Segnatura, have become known all over the world through millions of reproductions. In her handbook *The Vatican*, before World War I a must for everyone visiting Rome, Mary Knight Potter gives her generation's estimate of both Raphael and Michelangelo:

The Stanza della Segnatura may be said to represent Raphael as does the Sistine Chapel Michelangelo. . . . In no other one work is the entire man of each so fully displayed. For clear, shining sanity, the Camera is unexcelled, while the Sistine exerts power and impressiveness attained by no other. In pure beauty and a unique perfection of decorative and mural composition, the Camera must take precedence. In the Sistine it is not beauty so much as it is an overpowering grandeur of conception that strikes one. The two cannot be compared. They are as dissimilar as a deep inland lake dazzling in its glorious shimmering blue and the restless, whirling waves of the ocean itself.

The author seems to prefer Raphael's sweetness to Michelangelo's *terribilità*. Michelangelo has always met with opposition, especially as a painter. When his *Last Judgment* was unveiled in the Sistine Chapel in 1551, there were many outcries of anger. Paul IV would have liked to cover up the whole fresco but, as a compromise, merely ordered Daniele da Volterra to clothe the most conspicuous naked figures. Daniele gained for this the nickname *"Il Braghettone,"* the breeches-maker. Michelangelo had been in his grave for more than thirty years when another pope, Clement VIII, wanted the *Judgment* painted out altogether and yielded only after a sharp protest from the artists' guild, the Academy of Saint Luke. To this very day it is not uncommon to meet people who would agree with William Hazlitt, who compared the *Last Judgment* to "an immense field of battle, or charnel house, strewed with carcasses and naked bodies. . . . The whole is a scene of enormous ghastly confusion, in which you can only make out quantity and number, and vast, uncouth masses of bones and muscles. It has the incoherence and distortion of a troubled dream, without the shadowiness."

As for Raphael, his next and last patron was Leo X. In Raphael's celebrated portrait of him (now in the Uffizi), Leo is seen as a bloated man with a flabby face, weak eyes, and an unusually large head on a short neck. This Medici, who was only thirty-seven when he was elected to the pontifical chair, was, in his love of science, literature, and art, a true son of Lorenzo the Magnificent. He often neglected the duties of the Church, sold cardinals' hats, created new offices in order to sell them to the highest bidder, borrowed huge sums from bankers, and even pawned palace furniture, table plate, and jewels to obtain the vast sums of money he needed for his decorative and architectural tasks. But he was Raphael's most ardent patron—a highly cultured man, an excellent musician, and a shrewd politician.

"Let us enjoy the papacy since God had given it to us," is a remark attributed to Leo. It is fair to say that giving more and more commissions to Raphael was one of his major enjoyments. Leo had him design what is now known as "Raphael's Bible," a series of frescoes for a long arcaded passage in the Vatican. These paintings, with the exception of four that deal with Christian themes, are based on the Old Testament and were for the most part executed by Raphael's assistants. He had need of assistants, for in the

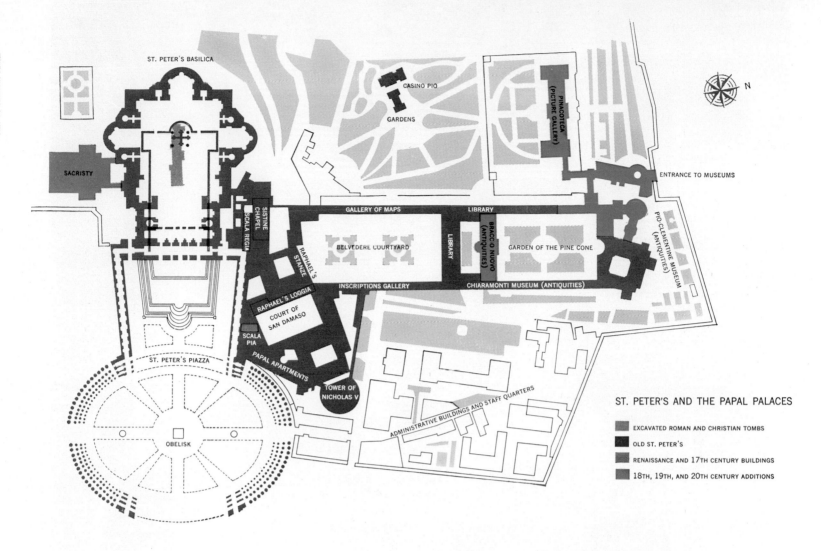

MAP BY MARTHA BLAKE

ST. PETER'S BASILICA

CASINO PIO

GARDENS

PINACOTECA (PICTURE GALLERY)

N

SACRISTY

ENTRANCE TO MUSEUMS

SISTINE CHAPEL

SCALA REGIA

GALLERY OF MAPS

LIBRARY

RAPHAEL'S STANZE

BELVEDERE COURTYARD

LIBRARY

BRACCIO NUOVO (ANTIQUITIES)

GARDEN OF THE PINE CONE

PIO-CLEMENTINE MUSEUM (ANTIQUITIES)

INSCRIPTIONS GALLERY

CHIARAMONTI MUSEUM (ANTIQUITIES)

RAPHAEL'S LOGGIA

COURT OF SAN DAMASO

SCALA PIA

PAPAL APARTMENTS

ST. PETER'S PIAZZA

TOWER OF NICHOLAS V

ADMINISTRATIVE BUILDINGS AND STAFF QUARTERS

OBELISK

ST. PETER'S AND THE PAPAL PALACES

EXCAVATED ROMAN AND CHRISTIAN TOMBS

OLD ST. PETER'S

RENAISSANCE AND 17TH CENTURY BUILDINGS

18TH, 19TH, AND 20TH CENTURY ADDITIONS

seven years that he served Leo X, Raphael did more work than many another does in a whole lifetime.

Bramante, before his death in 1514, especially requested that Raphael be made his successor as chief architect of St. Peter's. Yet Raphael, always ready to oblige, to disperse his immense creative powers, left little mark on St. Peter's. The building went very slowly. There was much opposition to the new venture. Many Romans would have preferred having the old basilica repaired instead of seeing vast sums squandered on an ambitious new scheme. In a satirical dialogue published in 1517, Bramante is refused entrance to Heaven by Saint Peter for having participated in the destruction of the old church. The architect defends himself by saying that Pope Leo is building a new one:

Saint Peter: "Well, then you must wait at the gate of Paradise until it is finished."

Bramante: "But if it never is finished?"

The anonymous writer shared the conviction of thousands who felt that the popes had embarked upon a project too large for men to finish. Leo X and Raphael had been dead for more than twenty years when Paul III, determined to delay the matter no longer, urged Michelangelo to take over the unfinished task and gave him full freedom to enlarge or transform the whole according to his own conception. Michelangelo discarded Raphael's design and went back to Bramante's plan of a temple in the shape of a Greek cross; but instead of the hemispherical Pantheon-type dome conceived by Bramante, he designed another one, slightly narrower but of much greater height, more "Mannerist," more dynamic. Michelangelo died in 1564 leaving the dome unfinished, and it was not completed until 1590. While it does not differ much from Michelangelo's plan, neither he nor his predecessor Bramante would have recognized the outer shape of St. Peter's as it finally emerged under the architect Carlo Maderna in the beginning of the seventeenth century. To enlarge its capacity, he extended the building toward the front, giving it the shape of a Latin cross.

There was a final flowering of art and architecture on the right bank of the Tiber when those two energetic figures of the Baroque age, Urban VIII and Giovanni Lorenzo Bernini, met and decided they were made for each other: the Pope, vain and extroverted, but also enterprising; and the sculptor, highly gifted, but without the depth of a Michelangelo—a man whose greatest talent lay, as one of his biographers put it, in "bringing out the picturesque."

Urban (1623–1644), a member of the Barberini family,

*S*t. Peter's dome towers high over Bernini's baldacchino, which itself rises 95 feet above the great altar. This picture was taken from the foot of one of the baldacchino's four twisted columns, which derive from the columns in Constantine's basilica (see painting on pages 30–31).

TEMPLA DOMVM EXPOSITIS:VICOS FORA MOENIA PONTES:
VIRGINEAM TREVII QVOD REPARARIS AQVAM.
PRISCA LICET NAVTIS STATVAS DARE COMMODA PORTVS:
ET VATICANVM CINGERE SIXTE IVGVM:
PLVS TAMEN VRBS DEBET:NAM QVAE SQVALORE LATEBAT:
CERNITVR IN CELEBRI BIBLIOTHECA LOCO.

The Vatican Library's greatest patron was Sixtus IV, who endowed it in 1475 and opened it to scholars—making it the first public library in Europe. The Melozzo da Forlì fresco opposite shows Sixtus receiving a new librarian, attended by his nephews (the one in red became Julius II). The library's treasures included priceless church archives like the eighteenth-century letter files at the right. Below are its largest and smallest books: a thirteenth-century Old Testament and, on top of it on the tiny pedestal, a minute sixteenth-century missal.

is remembered as the last pope to practice nepotism on a grand scale. Yet it was also he who acknowledged the genius of Galileo, reluctantly allowed the Inquisition to compel Galileo's abjuration, later gave him a pension, and finally tendered him the last sacrament. He was also one of the few among the later popes to embellish Rome with superb buildings. It was his great distinction, on November 18, 1626, one hundred and twelve years after Bramante's death, to consecrate the completed St. Peter's.

In most respects the façade was as it appears today. But within the church, beneath the dome, there was still a vast, empty space. Bernini, not yet thirty but already famous, was called upon. Between 1624 and 1633 he built the huge *baldacchino*, with its twisted baroque columns, that today shelters the altar. There was not enough bronze for this fantastic canopy, so the Pope ordered his men to strip the roof of the Pantheon. This led one Roman to compose a bitter epigram: *"Quod non fecerunt barbari, fecerunt Barberini"* ("What the barbarians failed to do, the Barberini did").

Bernini did not do well under Innocent X, but he prospered under another pope, Alexander VII, a scholar who loved to coin epigrams and bandy Latin quotations with humanist friends (he left the affairs of state to his secretaries). He was a man with great aesthetic insight: he sensed that there was something missing in front of the church, and he knew that Bernini would find the solution. To give shape to the piazza, to shut out the adjacent hodgepodge of buildings, and to create a gesture of welcome to pilgrims, Bernini constructed two great elliptic galleries supported by four rows of columns. The length of this piazza is 366 yards, and the greatest width between the colonnades 260 yards.

The Città del Vaticano has indeed changed artistically

and architecturally in the past three centuries. There is not a single pontiff who did not order some room altered or some office building added. The popes are ardent collectors of art to this very day, though there could hardly be a greater difference than that between the Renaissance hedonist Leo X and a modern man like Leo XIII, the nineteenth-century "socialist pontiff" known for his vigorous championship of the rights of the workingman. What most of the modern popes have done is to build new homes for existing collections rather than to acquire new objects. In particular, new halls were added, such as the Sala a Croce Greca (hall in the form of a Greek cross), built by the architect Simonetti for Pius VI (1775-1799), to house the celebrated porphyry sarcophagi of Saint Helena and Saint Constantia, the mother and half-sister of Constantine the Great. The same architect designed the Sala Rotonda, with a cupola in the style of the Pantheon, which houses such sculptures as the superb portrait of Nerva and the colossal statue of Antinoüs, Hadrian's favorite who drowned in the Nile and was subsequently deified by the Emperor. Simonetti also built the octagonal Sala delle Muse, named for the Hellenistic statues of Muses surrounding Apollo playing the cithara. To the same period belongs the Sala degli Animali, so called for its collection of animal statuary in white and colored Greek or Roman marble.

The Vatican Art Gallery was a creation of Pius XI; the collection had no fixed home until he opened the Pinacoteca Vaticana in 1932, but its origins go back as far as Paul II (1464-1471), a Venetian who brought small Greek panel paintings with him to the Vatican. The most striking picture in the collection is the huge *Transfiguration*, one of Raphael's last works. Unfinished at the time of his death,

TEXT CONTINUED ON PAGE 48

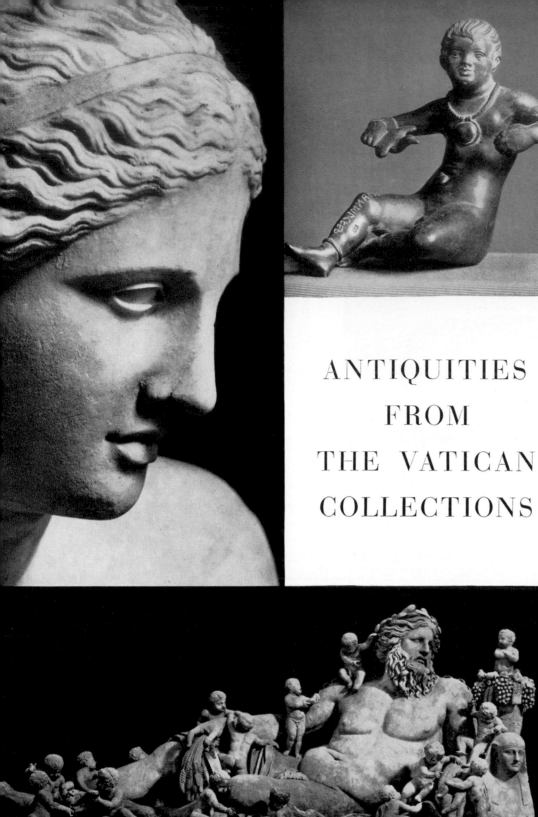

ANTIQUITIES
FROM
THE VATICAN
COLLECTIONS

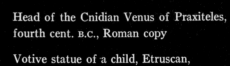

Clockwise from top left:

Head of the Cnidian Venus of Praxiteles,
fourth cent. B.C., Roman copy

Votive statue of a child, Etruscan,
third cent. B.C.

The Emperor Augustus, Roman,
first cent. A.D.

Sarcophagus with myth of Alcestis, Roman

Head of Minerva, Roman mosaic

Head of a horse, Etruscan

The Nile, Hellenistic, Roman copy

Clockwise from top left:

Ajax and Achilles, Athenian vase, sixth cent. B.C.

Belvedere Apollo, fourth cent. B.C., Roman copy

A Roman couple, third cent. A.D.

Queen Arsinoë, Egyptian, third cent. B.C.

The Discobolus of Myron, fifth cent. B.C., Roman copy

Detail of the Laocoön, Hellenistic, first cent. B.C.

TEXT CONTINUED FROM PAGE 45

the lower part was completed by his pupils. Leonardo da Vinci's *Saint Jerome* was the discovery of the well-known collector Cardinal Fesch, who at the beginning of the last century found it serving as the lid of a chest; the head, which was missing, was later found by the Cardinal in a shoemaker's shop, and the reconstructed picture was eventually purchased by Pius IX. Most of the pictures are Italian and treat religious subjects. There was never much methodical purchasing, and some of the paintings are tedious or of inferior quality. But the Raphael and the Da Vinci, such masterpieces as Titian's *Madonna di San Niccolò dei Frari* and Caravaggio's *Entombment*, and notable works by Giotto, Vivarini, Pinturicchio, Perugino, and other early Renaissance artists, make it a collection that would be the glory of any place less richly endowed than the Vatican.

Here, however, it is overshadowed not only by the frescoes but by the world's largest collection of Greco-Roman statuary. The Vatican's most celebrated sculpture is perhaps the Laocoön. Next in fame is that graceful youth, the Apollo Belvedere; our grandfathers believed it to be an original from the great fourth century B.C., whereas we have come to realize that it is only a Roman copy of that work (though a superb one). The noblest piece of sculpture, however, is not among the thousands of pieces in the Vatican museum collections but in St. Peter's, in a chapel on the right side not far from the entrance. It is Michelangelo's *Pietà*. He was only twenty-four when he carved it out of marble, yet it has the true mark of genius and a perfection independent of age. Nobody has succeeded in producing such tension out of the juxtaposition of the dead Christ's rigidity and the Madonna's graceful flowing robes, or in dramatizing pain by little more than the mother's slight inclination of the head. All the great frescoes, all the huge panels and canvases, all the precious antique statues, pale beside this work. There is a legend that Michelangelo signed it—the only work he ever signed—after having overheard some northern visitors attributing it to their own countrymen. But it is more likely that the inscription *"Michaelangelus Buonarotus Florentin Faciebat"* on the broad band running across the left breast and shoulder of the Madonna was indicative of the young man's justifiable pride. Whatever he may have produced before, from now on everything would be distinctively "Michelangelo."

The simple fisherman from Galilee, said to be buried beneath the basilica named for him, would feel uneasy in this city of twenty thousand rooms called the Vatican, to say nothing of St. Peter's, with its seven hundred and seventy-seven columns, forty-four altars, and nearly four hundred statues. His eyes would be blinded by the gleam of the polished travertine on the façade, overwhelmed by the marble and gold inside. He might feel like the servant woman in Franz Werfel's *Embezzled Heaven*, into whose head the author puts this observation:

This was less a church of the Crucified One than the proud royal palace of an omnipotent God, a place in which to hold brilliant court here below. It seemed as if in this supreme throne room the whole of humanity would find space to approach the steps of the Monarch of Heaven and His vicar on earth. Thousands were lost in its vastness, and even tens of thousands did not suffice to fill all the transepts, chapels, niches, and corners.

But the Apostle would also be moved by the knowledge that so many gifted men through the centuries have devoted their talent, inclinations, and even passions toward constructing this splendid church and toward making the Vatican the greatest artistic treasure house of Christendom.

Alfred Werner is a contributing editor of Arts *and the U.S. correspondent of* Pantheon, *an international magazine of art.*

GEORGINA MASSON—FROM *Rome for Ourselves,* McGRAW HILL, NEW YORK, THAMES & HUDSON, LONDON

ANDERSON

O ne of the most enduring symbols of the continuity of the Vatican is the Roman bronze pine cone (left) that once stood before Constantine's basilica. The growing magnificence of church and palace, and a desire to retreat from it occasionally, may have led Pius IV to build in 1562 his charming garden villa, the Casino Pio (right). Or perhaps he only wanted to get away from the noise: Michelangelo's dome, serene and solid now in the distance, was under construction during most of Pius's reign.

48

The Multiple
ROBERT GRAVES

By PETER QUENNELL

Robert Graves in Majorca, 1961

government university. The salary attached was fourteen hundred pounds per annum—a huge sum by the poet's modest standards, so huge that it emboldened him to suggest that a young American poetess of the day, Laura Riding Gottschalk, with whom he had established contact (I think through another American poet, John Crowe Ransom), should leave home, cross the Atlantic, and join the Graves family on their Near Eastern pilgrimage.

Thus began a momentous literary partnership that lasted until 1939, and of which the opening stages are allusively celebrated in the postscript to Graves's autobiographical volume, while its conclusion is briefly mentioned in his preface to *The Common Asphodel*. Laura Riding, as she soon renamed herself, was—and no doubt still is—a decidedly formidable personage, whose influence over the friends and disciples she gathered round her can only be compared to that of Mme de Staël over the little group at Coppet. Physically, too, there may have been some likeness. Both were shockheaded, square-built women, with large powerfully compulsive eyes; both excited alarm as well as respect and were treated by their admiring associates with all the deference due to a contemporary sibyl. In 1929, the autobiographer notes, "Nancy and I suddenly parted company." By that time, he had also parted with most of the "leading and subsidiary characters" depicted in *Good-bye to All That;* and, having cleared the stage, he embarked on a new relationship that dominated his life and work for several years to come. Its setting, until the outbreak of the Spanish Civil War, was the island of Majorca and subsequently a small château in the north of France and a farm near New Hope, Pennsylvania.

Simultaneously his verse grew more sparse and austere, his critical prose writings more prophetic and dogmatic in tone. Every genuine poet seems to incorporate several contrasted but complementary selves; and besides the Imaginative Artist, Robert Graves's make-up includes the Quirky Pedant and the Wild-eyed Prophet, the last presumably a relic of his Celtic inheritance, while the Pedant obviously derives from his learned German forebears. Like D. H. Lawrence, in his search for a new society he was constantly groping toward a new religion; and at this stage, when he had bidden farewell to the past, his utterances were sometimes profoundly obscure, even unexpectedly pretentious— witness the enigmatic paragraphs with which he brings to an end the story of his early life. Ordinary events acquired a transcendental significance. I remember, for example, how one day I happened to meet William Nicholson in the street outside his studio. He looked gloomy. "We've just had a postcard from Robert and Laura, to say that they are leaving for Spain together to *stop Time,*" he reported, with a dubious shake of the head.

Yet, if the influence of Laura Riding accentuated his prophetic tendency—and if the prophet's pronouncements were apt to be rather dark and tangled—it also impelled

ERIC KENNINGTON

The drawing above is of young Graves the Soldier; the autobiographical poem below represents Graves the Poet.

MY NAME AND I

The impartial Law enrolled a name
    For my especial use:
My rights in it would rest the same
Whether I puffed it into fame
    Or sank it in abuse.

Robert was what my parents guessed
    When first they peered at me,
And *Graves* an honourable bequest
With Georgian silver and the rest
    From my male ancestry.

They taught me: 'You are *Robert Graves*
    (Which you must learn to spell),
But see that *Robert Graves* behaves,
Whether with honest men or knaves,
    Exemplarily well.'

Then though my I was always I,
    Illegal and unknown,
With nothing to arrest it by—
As will be obvious when I die
    And *Robert Graves* lives on—

I cannot well repudiate
    This noun, this natal star,
This gentlemanly self, this mate
So kindly forced on me by fate,
    Time and the registrar;

And therefore hurry him ahead
    As an ambassador
To fetch me home my beer and bread
Or commandeer the best green bed,
    As he has done before.

Yet, understand, I am not he
    Either in mind or limb;
My name will take less thought for me,
In worlds of men I cannot see,
    Than ever I for him.

him to sharpen the edge of his style, to think more deeply and carefully about the exact value of the words he used in verse; and it was counterbalanced by his instinctive affection for vivid, concrete, sensuous images. Laura Riding's intellectualism, often somewhat arid in her own poems, helped to remove from his verse the last touches of Georgian sentimentalism. But neither poetry nor prophecy could settle his economic problem; and from 1934 onwards he published his famous series of historical novels, beginning with *I, Claudius* and *Claudius the God,* of which the former was awarded the Hawthornden and the James Tait Black Memorial prizes. But the poet was always incensed should the novelist receive undue attention. He dismissed his best-selling novels as potboilers, written chiefly with the object of producing a quick financial dividend.

That they are much more than that, every reader will agree; though again and again he may find himself disputing Robert Graves's interpretations of the past. Personally, I have always thought of the Roman Empire as an immense, complex, inhuman but on the whole harmonious and smooth-running piece of bureaucratic mechanism, which continued to operate efficiently even at times when a sadistic madman —a Tiberius, a Caligula, or a Nero—happened to occupy the Palatine Hill; during the reign of Nero, I believe, the Roman provinces were particularly well-administered. Graves prefers to emphasize the human element, with all its individual waywardness. His Romans have a faintly rustic air: beneath the fringe of the purple-bordered toga we glimpse a pair of hobnailed boots, and in his text the meetings of the Senate are apt to suggest the confabulations of an Oxfordshire Rural District Council. His generals are English infantry officers, and the Emperor Claudius, whom he chose as the hero of his first two books, was one of the homeliest and crankiest members of his tragic and eccentric family.

Not content with re-creating the past through the medium of imaginative fiction, Graves has also developed a taste for revising, refurbishing, and rewriting the literary records that it left behind. He is among the foremost rewriters of the age—here the Pedant and the Prophet combine their efforts. In 1933 he published *The Real David Copperfield,* illustrating how Dickens *might,* and *ought to,* have designed his masterpiece, had he been unimpeded by Victorian social conventions; in 1953—a yet more ambitious effort— he "restored" *The Nazarene Gospel,* a revised version of the New Testament, stripped of tendentious Pauline glosses; and in 1955 came the turn of *The Greek Myths,* to which he endeavored to give back their ancient simplicity and dignity of meaning, with the help of the abstruse wisdom he had imbibed at the footstool of the White Goddess. The focal point of all his scholarly researches is the bizarre theory of "analeptic thought," based on his belief that forgotten events may be recovered by the exercise of intuition, which affords

sudden glimpses of truth "that could not have been arrived at by inductive reasoning." In practice, of course, this sometimes means that the historian first decides what he would *like* to believe, then looks around for facts to suit his thesis. According to a classical scholar I once consulted, although Graves's facts themselves are usually sound, they do not always support the elaborate conclusions he proceeds to draw from them: two plus two regularly make five or six, and genuine erudition and prophetic imagination conspire to produce some very odd results.

Certainly *The White Goddess* is a strange and perplexing volume—a bold attempt to dethrone Apollo and Zeus and the poetic standards they exemplify in favor of a much more venerable divine ruler, the Mediterranean Mother Goddess, prototype of the Muse whom every "Chief Poet" serves with a mixture of exaltation and alarm. The young poet who ceases to write verse, Graves goes on to suggest, may have forfeited his literary birthright because he has lost his sense of that formidable divinity: "the woman whom he took to be a Muse, or who was a Muse, turns into a domestic woman and would have him turn similarly into a domesticated man. . . . The White Goddess is anti-domestic; she is the perpetual 'other woman,' and her part is difficult indeed for a woman of sensibility to play for more than a few years, because the temptation to commit suicide in simple domesticity lurks in every maenad's and muse's heart."

Whatever its limitations may be as a work of historical research or literary scholarship—one is surprised to learn that only two English writers, John Skelton and Ben Jonson, deserve to be considered "Chief Poets"; and there is an unfortunate slip at the beginning of Chapter Twenty-five about the Aztecs and the Incas—*The White Goddess* will prove an invaluable source book for all who wish to study the writer's personal development and hope to understand his poetry. In his opening sentence he makes a proud claim: "Since the age of fifteen poetry has been my ruling passion and I have never intentionally undertaken any task or formed any relationship that seemed inconsistent with poetic principles. . . . Prose has been my livelihood, but I have used it as a means of sharpening my sense of the altogether different nature of poetry, and the themes that I choose are always linked in my mind with outstanding poetic problems." That claim, I think, is perfectly justified, at least insofar as it concerns his single-minded, lifelong devotion to the art of poetry; for, if Robert Graves now stands high above the great majority of modern English poets, he owes his position not only to his inherited gifts but to the remarkable persistence and diligence with which he has exploited them. He has turned out an enormous quantity of prose, much of it extremely good prose; yet it is difficult to imagine him as anything but a professional poet, whose sheer professionalism is no less conspicuous than the imaginative zeal with which he serves his art. We may discount a good deal of his pedantic and prophetic theorizing: his volume of collected verse remains, and his poems speak their own language.

Today Robert Graves is sixty-six (he was born in 1895), a tall, robust, grizzle-headed figure, with a broken nose, like Michelangelo's, and a grayish-pallid, untanned Northern skin. He has remarried and founded a new family; but he still lives on the rocky shores of Majorca, in the stone-walled, tile-roofed house that he designed and built himself some thousand feet above the sea. Behind it the mountains rise up steep and grim, and around the house is a grove of fragrant orange and lemon trees. Nearby, a smaller house shelters his secretary, Karl; and the *posada* in the village, which also belongs to him, often accommodates visiting friends and admirers. Though much more spacious than it was at Islip, his way of life is unextravagant. At least, he works extraordinarily hard; and although a saucepan on the hob no longer shares his attention with his books and manuscripts, he still writes in furious bursts of energy, often leaving his desk to pace the floor or wander through the house and garden.

His talk is vigorous and idiosyncratic, usually prefaced by a bold assertion concerning the "real truth," as he sees it, about some question of topical or historical interest; for, like Sir Thomas Browne, he is much preoccupied with putting right the "vulgar errors" of our age.

Incidentally, he is a believer in signs and portents. He has never lost his sense of mystery, his instinctive feeling for the numinous; and he uses the Islamic word *báraka*, as he explained some months ago in a paper read at a meeting of the American Academy of Arts and Letters, to denote the natural magic that may distinguish "almost anything," from a battered old metal cooking pot to a modern poem or the King James Bible.

Just as the Bible in the latest English version has been purged of its antique numinous quality, so he finds that the twentieth-century world is gradually losing its primitive sense of wonder. In his own poetry that sense of wonder persists—wonder combined with delight and dread. Like every true imaginative artist, he shows us trees as men, and men as trees walking, and helps to break down the rigid conceptual pattern imposed on the ordinary unpoetic mind by years of lethargy and acquiescent habit. Again, like every good poet, he has both an individual view of existence and a correspondingly individual style. "Genuine modernists [he has written] do not make individual style their object: they try to write each poem in a way which fits it best. But the sum of their work has individuality because of their natural variousness. . . . True style is the personal handwriting in which poetry is written; if it can be easily imitated or reduced to a formula it should be at once suspect to the poets themselves."

Robert Graves, as a writer of verse, is both unusually various and unusually flexible. Perhaps the variety is most apparent; in the paperback edition of his collected verse that I have recently been looking through, I see that I have marked at random poems on Odysseus, a butterfly, the art of storytelling, war memories, the Priapic principle, lovers' speech, deception in love, cat-goddesses, snow, bears, the Majorcan sirocco, and the communiqué that Persian press officers probably issued about the Persian failure to conquer Greece—the last inspired, I am told, by the British failure to land at Dieppe during an early stage of World War I.

Here the "natural variousness" of the poet's mind produces without question an effect of stylistic individuality. Yet, although each poem is a separate unit existing in its own right, together these units form a continuous record of the poet's extended mental odyssey, from an English Ithaca, the scene of his childhood, through the devastating storms of war, past perilous Circean islets and onward across still troubled waters. Odysseus did not expect that he would reach his final goal; nor presumably does Robert Graves. Meanwhile he continues to keep a log, written up (he tells us) "at the fairly constant rate" of four or five poems a year since 1914. The record is lyrical yet never devoid of wit: he employs wit as successfully as the seventeenth-century English poet; and he, too, is personal and satirical without impairing his persuasive lyric flow.

If we are to enjoy him as he deserves to be enjoyed—and the merits of a poem can only be gauged by the quality and the duration of the pleasure it arouses—his poems should be read in bulk. A survivor of the *Georgian Poetry* period, he alone among his immediate contemporaries—and, indeed, among representatives of the postwar literary age—has contrived to hold a steady onward course. At no point is its line broken, as the lines of the human palm are broken; his poetic "Line of Destiny" is astonishingly straight and clear. The ghosts have receded, though they have not completely vanished; love, always an obsessive preoccupation, continues to excite his analytical instincts, as it once excited those of Donne; and this "near-honourable malady" is the subject of many of his latest poems.

How much does he owe to World War I? By overcoming that traumatic experience, he gained the strength and the sense of direction he needed; and he himself seemed to acknowledge the debt he owed when he visited London in 1961. Interviewed by a vagrant journalist, he sent up the customary controversial kite. What was wrong with Europe and America today? The younger generation, he suggested, was subconsciously looking forward to, and feeling the lack of, yet another international conflict.

Peter Quennell is co-editor of the English magazine History Today, *and the author of a number of literary biographies, critical studies, and historical essays. He wrote the article on Charles James Fox in the May, 1960, issue of* Horizon.

The Disappearance of Don Juan

What the moral indignation of three centuries
could not achieve, our own age has done: the
Don is dead, not because we are too puritanical
for him, but because we are too licentious

By HENRY ANATOLE GRUNWALD

Madamina! Il catalogo è questo
Delle belle che amò il padron mio . . .
In Italia seicento e quaranta,
In Alemagna duecento e trent'una,
Cento in Francia, in Turchia novant'una,
Ma, ma in Ispagna, son già mille e tre!
V'han fra queste contadine,
Cameriere, cittadine;
V'han contesse, baronesse,
Marchesane, principesse,
E v'han donne d'ogni grado,
D'ogni forma, d'ogni età!

            • • •

Pentiti!
No! *   *—Don Giovanni

We think of our literature, no less than of our age, as loose and lascivious. Sex appears to be rampant. Writers treat it with a freedom and a wealth of detail which in other periods were permitted only to pornographers. We regard ourselves as a pretty wicked lot, and yet amid all this wickedness a strange fact—or, rather, a strange lack—stands out: Don Juan is nowhere in sight. The archlibertine has left the revels. His name remains in our language, but the character behind the name has disappeared. Since Shaw's *Man and Superman,* in 1903, no major work of fiction or drama has centered around the Don Juan figure. Seduction, adultery, fornication, rape, are readily found, but not Don Juanism with its characteristic dash of heroics and gay defiance. We can no more expect a true Don Juan in our literature than we expect to find a character with a cloak and sword at our next cocktail party, singing *"Là ci darem la mano"* to the pretty Vassar girl in the corner.

Among other things, of course, Don Juan is a myth. But as mythological figures go (compared, for instance, to the White Goddess, or Prometheus, or Ulysses, or Faustus, or Tristan), the Don is a newcomer. His existence and his meaning depend on a certain attitude toward love, and love is a relatively modern invention.

In antiquity the relations between men and women consisted mostly of frank sensuality or of domestic comfort. Love mixed with passion was considered a form of madness —and one afflicting women more often than men. Nor did the advent of Christianity, the religion of love, herald love in anything like its modern sense. For many centuries Christianity fought to subdue an unruly, violent, and still strongly pagan world to Christian laws in all matters, including sex. Carnal desire, even within marriage, was considered, at best, a necessary evil. Thus the concept of romantic love was completely alien both to what might be called the pagan underground and to the dominant Christian order. When romantic love made its startling appearance in the eleventh century, through the works and visions of the troubadours, it became a major revolutionary force—a revolution of belief, feeling, and behavior, not to mention literature, compared to which

the Renaissance, as C. S. Lewis has observed, was a mere surface ripple.

In literature the revolution replaced the great epic themes of war, of faith, and of nature and made love between man and woman the center of the story-telling art. In life the revolution established love both beyond mere sexual enjoyment and beyond Christian-feudal ideas of marriage. In the elaborate patterns of courtly love the traditional role of woman was reversed; instead of dominating and using her, man treated her with abject humility and served her as if she were his feudal lord and he her vassal. He glorified her to a blasphemous degree, and courtly love, in effect, developed a rival religion to Christianity.

Whether or not it was, as has been suggested, a highly refined form of paganism rebelling against Christianity's moral order, courtly love glorified adultery. It held that love existed only outside the mundane, practical concerns of marriage. A famous ruling handed down in 1174 by a "court of love" under the patronage of the Countess of Champagne held that "love cannot extend its right over two married persons" because true love must be given freely, while in marriage it is given as a matter of duty and constraint.†

It is not entirely clear to what extent this glorification of adultery was theoretical or how far it went in practice. There is no doubt that courtly love professed chastity—or at least moderation—as ranking high among its ideals. When one troubadour sang, "I approve that my lady should long make me wait and that I should not have from her what she promised," he may have been expressing the insight that it is desire, not fulfillment, which is love's best part. Or he may have been driving at a more mystical meaning. In an

---

* "Little lady, this is the catalogue / Of the beauties my master has loved . . . / In Italy six hundred and forty, / In Germany two hundred and thirty-one, / A hundred in France, in Turkey ninety-one, / But in Spain there are already one thousand and three! / Amongst these there are peasant girls, / Chambermaids, townswomen; / There are countesses, baronesses, / Marchionesses, princesses, / And there are women of every degree, / Every shape, every age! . . . Repent! / No!"

† See a discussion of this in "The Greatest of Courtly Lovers" by Morton M. Hunt, in Horizon for September, 1959.

Opposite: A nineteenth-century French costume design for the hero of Don Giovanni

ingenious analysis of the Tristan myth, Denis de Rougemont has pointed out that whenever the two lovers have an opportunity to settle down for a time to enjoy their passion, something happens to separate them—and the obstacles are often of their own making. This is so not only because the story must be kept going but because the ideal of courtly love demands it. That ideal, De Rougemont believes, was somehow linked to the Albigensian heresy, a movement of Manichean origin, which condemned both sexual intercourse and marriage as serving only to perpetuate a world intrinsically evil. Hence he sees in Tristan and Isolde not a desire for love's fulfillment but a desire for desire—kept alive by separation—and ultimately a desire for death.

Almost four centuries separate the heyday of courtly love and the first appearance of Don Juan—in Tirso de Molina's play *The Trickster of Seville and the Guest of Stone,* in 1630. In between lies the Renaissance, that titanic outburst of liberation as well as libertinage, of humanism as well as inhumanity, of man's glorification as well as woman's worship—the age of the passionate humanist, Petrarch, and the cynical amorist, Boccaccio. In a sense Don Juan is a Renaissance man, a character who might have walked out of the *Decameron.* But he assumes his true stature only when seen against the fading backdrop of courtly love. He is a kind of corruption of the troubadour, the exact opposite of Tristan. Courtly romances continued to hold the public imagination all

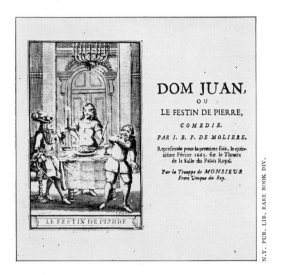

Molière's Dom Juan *first saw print under this title page, 17 years after its première in 1665.*

through the turbulence of the Renaissance era; more or less at the same time that the De Molina play appeared, all Europe was entranced by *L'Astrée,* a long and preposterous chronicle of the handsome shepherd Céladon and his involvements with druid priestesses, princesses, wood nymphs, shepherdesses, and the God of Love in person. Not much later Mlle de Scudéry, in her novel *Clélie,* invented *La Carte du Tendre,* or "The Map of Tenderness," in which—much in the spirit of the medieval courts of love—the whole territory of love was laid out. There were, among innumerable other localities, the Villages of Great Heart and Generosity; the river Attraction; the towns of Honesty, Obedience, and Constancy; and the Lake of Indifference. It is as a sneering opposite of Céladon, an invader tearing up the *Carte du Tendre,* that the original Don Juan makes his entrance.

According to legend Don Juan was a Spanish nobleman, assassinated by Franciscans who, in the words of one chronicler, wanted "to put an end to his excesses and blasphe-

mies." At any rate, the outline of Tirso de Molina's drama is familiar enough, and simple enough. In the course of three acts Don Juan uses up four women: two of them highborn and two from the lower orders. His technique is fairly unimaginative and standardized. He wins the society girls by impersonating their true suitors, and the two proletarian girls—one a fisherman's, the other a peasant's daughter—simply by promising to marry them. He is capable of intoxicating flattery and lyrical speeches with all of them; but if anything, he is more poetic with the simple girls than with the ladies. Fiancés or honorable suitors are readily bamboozled and enmeshed in all sorts of wicked complications. Fathers, guardians, and other figures of authority are brushed aside with equal ease, until Doña Ana's father, whom Juan has killed, returns to life in the stony guise of the famous statue and drags the Don to hell, and damnation.

Several things stand out in a re-examination of this old play. One, obviously, is Don Juan's lack of any real affection for the seduced women. He plans his getaway before beginning his conquest: "Why, for her love I'm almost dying. / I'll have her now, then scamper flying."

Unlike Tristan, or any other typical courtly lover, he is interested only in physical satisfaction and sneers at any suggestion of moderation or delay, let alone chastity. He shares the troubadour's low opinion of marriage, but for wholly different reasons. Where courtly love held marriage in contempt in order to idealize passion and glorify woman—in order, one might almost say, to establish the sacrament of romance—Don Juan brutally rejects romance along with marriage. Above all, he totally reverses the courtly lover's worship of woman: "In Seville / I'm called the Trickster; and my greatest pleasure / Is to trick women, leaving them dishonored."

Don Juan is thus in double rebellion, not only against convention and the Christian order, but against woman herself. He fights not only churchly morality but romantic love. Far from serving the lady, he uses and abuses her, vengefully reverting to a pagan, a Greek—an almost Oriental—disregard for woman as a soul-bearing human being.

From this obvious characteristic, two opposite conclusions have often been drawn. The romantics believe that Don Juan, perhaps once disappointed in love, endlessly searches for the ideal woman whom he can never find. The psychological cynics, on the other hand, believe that he really hates women and that in his perennial conquests he is trying to punish them. Both views seem exaggerated. Not a line in De Molina's drama suggests that he is looking for his dream girl. Nor does his contemptuous treatment of women carry a suggestion of hatred: revulsion from the meek courtly tradition, yes, but nothing so personal as hatred. Women are probably not important enough to him for that.

And yet he seems forever ready to risk his neck for them —in countless duels, scrapes, and ambushes. The answer to this seeming paradox must be that what Don Juan is willing to die for is not merely women, or even pleasure as such, but the very act of risk, the very freedom of tossing his life away if he so chooses. To face death for a worthwhile ideal is to play the game; to risk death for transient joys is to defy the game, to be contemptuous of life itself, to sneer at the human condition. Don Juan sees in death a gesture of defiance against human limitations, against the *status quo* in the universe, and against God himself.

If this makes Don Juan sound like an existentialist, a case can be made for the notion that he was. Albert Camus saw Don Juan as a man who does not hope for another life: "He gambles that other life against heaven itself. . . . He has but one reply to divine wrath, and that is human honor." He is an ordinary seducer for all that— "seducing is his condition in life"—but he knows it. He does not "collect" women, but "exhausts their number and with them his chances for life. . . . Don Juan has chosen to be nothing." Again and again the first Don Juan play asserts that

N.Y. PUB. LIB. MUSIC DIV.

The 1801 edition of Mozart's Don Giovanni *(première, Prague, 1787) depicts its climax.*

"what you have done, you pay for." Don Juan is willing to pay the price even of hell-fire. That is an act of rebellion against God closer to Faust's and Prometheus's than to that of the mere libertine. It is an act, moreover, compared to which the ravished virginity of a few women—or even of *mille e tre*—is relatively unimportant.

There is a clear hint in the play as to where this rebellion springs from: in his attitude toward the supernatural, Don Juan anticipates the dawning Age of Reason. After the statue has called on him, he is frightened but calms his fears by telling himself: "But all these things, / Begot by fear on the imagination, / Are quite unreal. To fear the dead is baseness." There speaks the rationalist mind, which even at the last moment seeks to strike down the phantom—the supernatural—with a sword. To the end, pride—human pride asserted against God and the universe—is Don Juan's dominant quality. When the statue offers him a meal of "tarantulas and vipers," he declares, "I shall eat it / Were all the snakes in hell upon one plate." The entire play contains exactly two lines of repentance, when Don Juan calls for a confessor; and this gesture is about as convincing as any moralistic ending tacked onto a Hollywood movie to appease the Legion of Decency.

To stress Don Juan's heroic insurrection against the supernatural is not to rob him, as Shaw did, of his sexuality and turn him into a mere metaphysical rebel. Both elements are interdependent and account for his fatal attractiveness. As a libertine without metaphysics, he would be a bore; as a metaphysician without his libertinage, he would (except for Shaw's wit) turn out merely a priggish liberal.

The intellectual distance between De Molina and Molière is great, but the core of the character has not changed in the latter's *Dom Juan, ou Le Festin de Pierre* (1665). The Molière play both simplifies and complicates the story: a few seductions have been removed; two vengeful brothers have been added; the comic servant, now called Sganarelle, has been built up; and a couple of typical Molière set pieces have been added—a duped creditor, two peasant girls wooed simultaneously. Not only has Don Juan become more amusing and unmistakably French—he has also become more of a hypocrite. He has actually married one of his women, Doña Elvira, and justifies his desertion of her with a dazzling show of Jesuitic reasoning. Above all he has become articulate; Molière's is the first Don Juan who really explains himself:

Would you have a man tie himself up to the first woman that captured his fancy, renounce the world for her, and never again look at anyone else? That *is* a fine idea, I must say, to make a virtue of faithfulness, to bury oneself for good and all in one single passion and remain blind ever after to all the other beauties that might catch one's eye! No! Let fools make a virtue of constancy! . . . Once one succeeds, what else remains?

This is the exquisitely cynical philosophy of the libertine, the philanderer's great charter, which went on to nourish the literature of gallantry in France and elsewhere. This particular speech, to be sure, omits the heroic, rebellious, heaven-defying side of the Don Juan character, but it is nevertheless very much in evidence elsewhere in the play. Molière's Don Juan, too, is a rationalist. He, too, rebels against the supernatural. After the statue first moves, he is momentarily frightened but recovers quickly: "Whatever it was, we will leave it at that. It is of no importance. We may have been deceived by a trick of light or overcome by some momentary giddiness which affected our vision." Later he adds: "There is certainly something there that I do not understand, but, whatever it is, it shall neither change my convictions nor shake my courage." And Molière's Don Juan is as unrepentant as the original. As he faces damnation at the statue's invitation, he once again announces his defiance: "Come what may, it shall never be said that I am the repenting sort."

In 1787, little more than one hundred and twenty years after Molière's play, appeared what remains undoubtedly the greatest Don Juan figure ever created in any of the arts, Mozart's *Don Giovanni*. In outline the libretto by Lorenzo da Ponte is not significantly different from earlier versions, although Da Ponte, a shrewd theatrical craftsman, added many stage tricks—masks, mistaken identities, abrupt and hilarious changes of mood. Effective though the libretto is, it is Mozart's music which superbly expresses the hero's nature, his extraordinary contradictions and ultimate tragedy. He is the character of whom the famous "catalogue aria" boasts so intoxicatingly (*"In Italia seicento e quaranta"*). He is also the character who can sing the ebullient, slightly coarse "champagne aria"— *"Finch' han dal vino"*—as well as the lovely, seductive *"Là ci darem,"* a sighing lyrical effusion. But above all he is the character who can prepare to receive the statue at dinner in the climactic scene, the scene that most perfectly epitomizes Don Giovanni's character. *"Io me voglio divertir,"* he announces with the arrogance of a crass hedonist ("I wish to amuse myself"). Yet in the music accompanying that line there is an unmistakably majestic strain, as there is during the farcical episodes involving food and the musicians. When the statue finally arrives, wreathed in unearthly music, Don Giovanni matches it in dignity, note for note. His order to his servant to open up—*"Apri!"*—shows no musical flicker of fear, nor does his reply to the statue's invitation: *"Ho fermo il core in petto: / Non ho timor, verrò!"* ("My heart is firm within my breast: / I am not afraid, I will come").

When his hand is already seized by the statue, his soul already in the clasp of hell, there is the great climactic clash: "Repent!" cries the statue, and *"No!"* replies the Don, unshaken and relentless, until the flames close in and a great scream of pain signals his damnation.

Mozart's is the last of the true Don Juans on stage or in literature. The eighteenth century provided a number of striking autobiographical Don Juans, including Casanova, who was more jolly rascal than hero, and the Marquis de Sade, who represents Don Juan's rebellion carried to insanity. But the protagonist of Tirso de Molina's play had been gradually romanticized by audiences who insisted on a happy ending. The most notable example of this revised and redemptive version of the story is *Don Juan Tenorio*, by José Zorrilla y Moral, first produced in 1844 and still widely performed in the Spanish-speaking world on All Saints' Day.

Juan is a young nobleman who makes a bet with a friend to see which of them, in the space of a year, can do more harm and seduce more women. Despite such exuberance, Juan wants to marry Doña Inés; but when her father finds out about the bet, he forbids the match and places Inés in a convent. Amid innumerable police chases and hairbreadth escapes, Don Juan abducts Inés—she happens to be unconscious at the time—and in almost the next breath seduces another girl, betrothed to his friend and betting partner, after which he kills Inés's father. The father's statuesque revenge is considerably more elaborate than in the original—for one thing, there is also a statue of Inés, who in the meantime has died of grief. But the really basic difference is that in the end Don Juan repents: already on his way to hell, he lifts a hand to heaven, and forgiveness sets in at once. In a final tableau the spirits of Doña Inés and Don Juan sink together on a bed of flowers scattered by angels.

This preposterous beatification was preceded by another even more significant transformation which robbed Don Juan of both God and devil, sentimentalized him, and made him, like the troubadours, subservient to woman. The change occurred, as Leslie Fiedler has pointed out, in Samuel Richardson's novel *Clarissa, or The History of a Young Lady* (1747–48). In it Don Juan appears as Robert Lovelace, an aristocrat, a libertine, and a rationalist with contempt for religion, convention (including marriage), and women. But there are some major differences. Where the original Don Juan appears to believe in God but defies him, Lovelace seems not to believe at all; the metaphysical essence of his rebellion therefore is changed. And where Don Juan moves from woman to woman, hardly remembering their names, Lovelace becomes obsessed with one woman alone.

The plot, entirely told in the form of letters, is intricate beyond Borgia politics, Dickensian novel, or American soap opera. Lovelace is supposed to marry Clarissa's older sister

Though Byron's Don Juan *was sardonic, here its rapt hero gazes at Julia.*

FROM Poetical Works of Byron, LONDON 1860's

but falls in love with the younger girl instead. Her parents, however, wish to marry her off to an elderly moneybags. When Clarissa refuses, she is held a virtual prisoner until Lovelace carries her off.

Disowned by her harsh father, Clarissa is at Lovelace's mercy, but manages to escape. After innumerable complications she is recaptured and returned to Lovelace, only to be drugged and raped by him. She manages to escape again, is falsely imprisoned for debt, released, and goes into a physical decline. Throughout all this, Lovelace is beginning to suspect that if he cannot have her any other way, he will have to marry her. But she buys her own coffin and makes up her mind to die. Her relations forgive her, but too late. She is buried in the family vault, while a heartbroken Lovelace goes to the Continent where he eventually provokes a duel with Clarissa's cousin and is mortally wounded. Dying, he hopes to expiate his crimes and calls on Clarissa: "Divine Creature! Fair Sufferer! Look down, Blessed Spirit, look down!"

Lovelace is clearly a Don Juan figure, but a very great change from the prototype is contained in one fact: Lovelace is defeated by woman. Where the terrible hand of the supernatural, the breath of hell itself, could not move the original Don Juan to repent, a woman extorts repentance from Lovelace. In the eyes of the readers Clarissa was clearly the winner and the heroine: when, in the installment publication of the novel, she finally died, church bells rang throughout all England.

LOUVRE-GIRAUDON

Delacroix painted the shipwreck that casts Byron's Don onto a Greek island and into a maiden's arms.

Part of the change in Don Juan is explained, of course, by the fact that Lovelace lives in a Protestant—and increasingly middle-class—society. Like the troubadours in the eleventh century, but for totally different reasons, the Protestant middle class in the eighteenth century re-established the superiority of the female. The Holy Virgin was discarded, but the virgin was regarded as almost holy. Despite a classic Christian belief that woman is the archtemptress, the source of sin, the Protestant middle class tended to see woman as pure and man as evil—a conviction still very much alive in the United States today. Also, it seems to have resented the cavalier attitude toward women, as it resented all aristocratic attitudes, countering leisure with thrift, nobility with diligence, combativeness with trade, paternalism with democracy, frivolity with sentimentality. In a sense, middle-class man needed woman to lean on because he felt insecure in the world. Where Latin-Catholic civilization used woman for procreation and delight, English-Prot-

estant civilization used her for procreation and uplift. In the Catholic tradition marriage is sanctioned not by love but by the law of God; adultery is a lesser sin than divorce —a comfortable situation for Don Juan. In the Protestant tradition marriage is indeed sanctioned by love as well as by law; divorce is not necessarily a sin at all, while adultery is—a highly inconvenient situation for Don Juan.

If in Richardson's treatment Don Juan succumbed to sentimentality, in Lord Byron's he escaped into humor. Appearing in 1819, more than half a century after Lovelace, Byron's Don Juan is once again an aristocrat and once again a rebel; in this immense and discursive work, in which digression seems to be the law of life and an aside may take a dozen stanzas, Byron castigates society, England, patriotism, power, money, women, poets, and almost anything that he was angry about. The work is a kind of limerick on an epic scale, ranging (as Mark Van Doren has put it) between the titanic and the cute.

In his satirical flights Byron's Don Juan is a figure to be reckoned with; but in his romantic escapades he is mostly a figure of fun. He is not a rebel against the supernatural, but only against human folly. The original Don Juan laughed, to be sure, but at the risk of death and damnation; Byron's Don Juan also laughs, but merely at the risk of offending respectability. Above all, Byron's hero is that modern oddity, a passive Don Juan—hence not a real Don Juan at all. Most of the time it is the women who pursue him, and it is he who allows himself to be taken. Among the types which the work satirizes are the era's Don Juans themselves, the lady-killers: "[Who] seem to say, 'Resist us if you can,' / Which makes a Dandy while it spoils a man."

Both Richardson's Lovelace, the repentant Don Juan who is ultimately defeated by woman, and Byron's passive Don Juan, who is seduced as much as seducer, jointly symbolize the fate of the Don Juan figure in much of the eighteenth and all of the nineteenth century; in other words, throughout the Age of the Novel. For the novel is essentially a female art form. It was not only the first art in history in which women distinguished themselves, but it was also addressed to a heavily female audience. The Seducer and the Persecuted Maiden continued their endless chase in countless stories, the more-or-less aristocratic villain relentlessly pursuing the pure bourgeois heroine; yet no matter what her fate, it is she who is the winner.

In the novel, as Bernard Shaw put it, Don Juan turned

into Doña Juana. The great rebels against society, against convention, even against the church, were all women. The three greatest heroines of the nineteenth-century novel, Becky Sharp, Emma Bovary, and Anna Karenina, who appeared within less than three decades of each other (1847–1875), were all fighters for a personal, emotional kind of independence, Furies avenging male inadequacy. Becky, in *Vanity Fair,* is an adventuress who uses up men the way Don Juan used up women, and survives them all. Emma Bovary may be a fool who comes to a tragic end, but that end can certainly not be blamed on male wickedness. Superficially Rodolphe looks like a Don Juan, but Emma is seduced by him only because she wishes to be. He and Léon, her other lover, are essentially the instruments of her obsessive quest for a different life. Similarly, Count Vronsky is not Anna Karenina's traducer: he may seem to be taking the initiative in the affair, but it is she who consents to it and pushes it to its doomed ending. He is more victim than she.

The world of the eighteenth- and the nineteenth-century novel, looking back as it does on the merrily licentious Restoration in England and on the heavily sensual Gallant Century in France, has its own libertine traditions. To judge from the novels, at least, men have love affairs constantly and discuss them freely. From the lavishly established semiofficial mistresses to the little flower girls and grisettes, adultery is a permanent, almost a respected institution. The point is not that the age lacks libertines but that the libertines lack the Don Juan spirit. There is an almost domestic tranquillity about many of these affairs, and always a certain lack of force on the part of the men as compared to great force on the part of their mistresses.

In short the image of man—even of the seducer—ultimately victimized by a female fate, applies not only to the stories of the Persecuted Maiden winning moral victories and the Misunderstood Wife bursting out of innumerable Doll Houses, it also applies to that third great category of the classic novel, the Glorified Courtesan. Triumphant or pathetic, genteel or vulgar, consumptive or peasant-strong, she gets the best of the men in the end—whether her name is Manon Lescaut, Carmen, Mme Marneffe, or Marguerite Gautier. The Lady of the Camellias may die pathetically, but how much more pathetic, and ridiculous, is her lover, Armand Duval, who when he learns that she will not see him again, swoons in the arms of his father. His is essen-

Les Trois Don Juans BY G. APOLLINAIRE, PARIS 1914

Goya based his Don and statue on Tirso de Molina's early drama.

tially the melancholy passivity of Goethe's young Werther, perhaps the ultimate reversal of the Don Juan figure, the lover who has lost any impulse to force from a woman what she will not give and is reduced to an abject, tearful, almost feminine (in the old sense) surrender to his destiny.

It cannot be said that the novel lacked strong, memorable male figures. They appear abundantly in Dickens, Tolstoy—particularly in *War and Peace*—Dostoevsky, and elsewhere. Most of the time they are made memorable, however, not by their relations with women, but through their involvement with other forces—war, wealth, conscience, and God. One remembers the Karamazovs not for Dimitri's or Fyodor's wenching but for Alyosha's tortured spiritual struggles. Raskolnikov is as little driven by sexuality (though he is redeemed by a woman) as is David Copperfield or Jean Valjean. And though closer to Don Juan, the adventurer-heroes of Stendhal's *The Red and the Black* and *The Charterhouse of Parma,* and their somewhat debased descendant in Guy de Maupassant's *Bel-Ami,* are all far more remarkable for their ambition than for their womanizing.

There is everywhere in the eighteenth- and the nineteenth-century novel the clink of coin and the rule of the balance sheet. Tragedy is seen in bankruptcy as much as in death. The fall of dynasties, as in *Buddenbrooks* and the *Forsyte Saga* (both nineteenth-century novels, although their date of publication narrowly puts them in the twentieth), is measured in flagging will but also in draining wealth. Nor is this preoccupation necessarily contemptible. If anything, nineteenth-century novelists underestimated the civilizing power of money, a power—going far beyond either thrift or greed—that transformed the world as no revolutionary force before it. The fact remains that in the traditional novel love is made along with money; no embrace is ever free from the shadow of financial success or failure; and the dowry, the business lawsuit, and the unpaid debt are the background of seduction. And this atmosphere does not suit Don Juan.

A man need not be rich to be a Don Juan, but he must be financially independent—either because he has enough money not to worry about it, or simply because he is not interested in what money can get him. He must have the aristocrat's essential contempt for wealth. For Don Juan to give up a conquest because it might cost too much, or to make another because it might bring gain, is absurd.

When Shaw finally approached the Don Juan story at

the turn of the century, he in a sense ratified the changes that had taken place during the Age of the Novel. Looking at society about him, he reports that man is no longer the pursuer, if he had ever been; woman is now in full pursuit. "The sex is aggressive, powerful: when women are wronged they do not group themselves pathetically to sing '*Protegga il giusto cielo!*': they grasp formidable legal and social weapons, and retaliate." Thus turning Don Juan Tenorio into Jack Tanner, he also turns him from hunter into quarry; and changing Doña Ana de Ulloa into Miss Anne Whitefield, he also changes her into a relentless goddess of the chase, who stops at no deceit, at no trick—not even the ultimate trick of feminine weakness at the crucial moment—to track down her man. She is the Life Force in petticoats, fulfilling nature's overriding purpose of perpetuating the race. Tanner can rant against his fate, but he can no more escape than a beetle in the teeth of a lizard, or any living thing in the grip of evolution.

Shaw goes further than this. He not only illustrates the re-ascendancy of woman in Western civilization; he also reports the near-overthrow of God. Jack Tanner is not only unable to conquer women because they conquer him, he is also unable to carry out his rebellion against God because that rebellion has become commonplace. What, in the day of the original Don Juan, was a brave and lonely act of defiance has become, at the beginning of the twentieth century, the commonplace skepticism of the crowd. Shaw's Don

Les Trois Don Juans BY G. APOLLINAIRE, PARIS 1914

In Zorrilla's 1844 version, Don Juan Tenorio, *the hero abducts Doña Inés.*

Juan can no longer be a rebel against the supernatural. But, being Shaw's creature, he is a rebel nonetheless—a rebel with a positive program. Since the majority is skeptical, argues Shaw in effect, the rebel against the majority must be affirmative. Tanner is a socialist and an advocate of selective breeding. His cause is the dream of the Superman.

Tanner's alter ego, the Don Juan whom Shaw presents only in the dream interlude set in hell, is still another reversal of the traditional Don Juan figure. Unlike the Jack Tanner of the play itself, he has become immune to women. Unlike Jack Tanner, he is scarcely even concerned with such practical matters as socialism. He is dedicated to intellectual contemplation. He is neither libertine nor romantic, neither hedonist nor rebel against God. "I tell you that in the pursuit of my own pleasure, my own health, my own fortune, I have never known happiness. It was not love for Woman that delivered me into her hands: it was fatigue, exhaustion." In short, Shaw's Don Juan is a moralist and

an ascetic, a sort of Nietzschean archangel—and more of a marble statue, except for his brilliant conversation, than The Statue itself.

Since Shaw, Don Juan has encountered what is his most trying time. The fact seems paradoxical, because perhaps in no other period of history has the preoccupation with sex been so intense and so widespread. The phenomenon is best illustrated by *Lady Chatterley's Lover,* written by a man who considered modern civilization insane and who dreamed of the natural life, of an unspoiled, unforced Eden. D. H. Lawrence was, among other things, a Rousseau of the four-letter word. But what makes his book remarkable, of course, are not those few Anglo-Saxon terms—poor, paltry, almost chaste compared to the vocabulary of a great many contemporary best sellers—but the overwrought lyricism of sexuality, which has done irreparable harm to a whole generation of writers who have learned from Lawrence not so much to call things by their right names (few will object to that) but to rhapsodize about sexual intercourse like overexcited and overeducated college girls.

It is, of course, not merely a matter of style. What Lawrence's language betrays, beyond the perfectly laudable desire to reproduce a human being's innermost reality, is an attempt to put sex through a mystical apotheosis. Sexual "fulfillment" becomes the only means of redeeming an otherwise empty life, of filling the spiritual void of modern existence. This whole attitude, of course, is entirely inimical to Don Juanism—as inimical as any other form of romanticism. The point is that the lover —exemplified in Lawrence's book by the celebrated gamekeeper—is expected to be masterful yet sweet, strong yet soft. This is basically a feminine ideal, and perhaps an admirable one; but it is not Don Juan's.

The theme of wicked seducer preying on pure maiden, of course, has continued to thrive in popular fiction, from Theodore Dreiser's *Sister Carrie,* where the seducer is no longer an aristocrat but a mere businessman named Hurstwood, who himself becomes a victim of a harsh and greedy society; to *Bertha, the Sewing Machine Girl* and innumerable other melodramas in which Don Juan, twirling a villainous mustache and swinging a menacing cane, becomes a broad caricature. But while the seduction theme remained indestructible, the balance of power between male and female continued to shift. Where Clarissa was clearly the stronger in the end, forcing her seducer to repentance, where

Becky Sharp was a rapacious Doña Juana, where even Emma Bovary was anything but an innocent victim, all these heroines and their nineteenth-century sisters were tender souls compared to the female monsters that increasingly populated modern fiction.

Whether or not these women accurately reflected reality, their literary creators obviously thought they did: Faulkner, Nathanael West, Hemingway, Wylie, and O'Hara, among others, specialized in the literature of the bitch. These were not merely forceful women seeking to ensnare a man; they went after their man with an almost masculine savagery, with a hunger obviously not destined ever to be appeased.

When faced with such women, what does a man—even a would-be Don Juan—do? There are really only two possibilities. He can knock them down; and this impulse helps account for a large strain of violent sex fiction, from the Marquis de Sade to Mickey Spillane, in which Don Juan has exchanged sword for blackjack or gun and uses the weapon not on his rivals but on the woman herself. Or else he can take flight; and this accounts for another strain of fiction which is not concerned with sex at all, or at least not primarily. A great many American writers have returned to the older themes of nature, of man contending with the elements, of warfare and male loyalties. This literary escape, of course, began with James Fenimore Cooper and Herman Melville—well before the female menace developed to its fullest in the Faulkner-West-O'Hara era. The western, rooted in Cooper but flourishing ever since, is an unmistakable escape from hag-ridden civilization. As for Melville, mere love or lust between men and women pales beside the monomaniac desire for revenge that animates *Moby Dick*. Hemingway, of course, has more to say about women; yet his romantic passages are usually his least convincing, and it can scarcely be an accident that the hero of *The Sun Also Rises* has been emasculated in the war. Hemingway was at his happiest as a writer when he spoke of the womanless world of guns and hunting, of companionship rather than love. The male loyalties and enmities in *For Whom the Bell Tolls* will always be more convincing that the preposterous sleeping bag scene ("the earth moved").

But American writers escaped woman not only in the wilderness but also in society. In Henry James and Edith Wharton, men have appetites and desires, but ultimately we see the cut of their clothes rather than the texture of

Sets for the 1949 production of Zorrilla's play were designed by Dali.

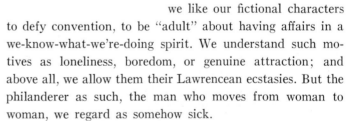

their flesh; and as often as not, the victories and defeats in these books occur not between man and woman or even man and man, but between family and family, tradition and tradition. John O'Hara, of course, fills his books with sex, regularly and almost dutifully, but the Don Juan spirit is excluded not only by the aggressiveness of the female but, more importantly, by the intense preoccupation with status. Ultimately O'Hara's men, to put it vulgarly, are more concerned with making the club or the team than the girl.

Despite these two streams of writing, in which the main preoccupation is not really sex, a mass of literature remains in which it is little or nothing else. Sometimes the emphasis is humorous: from Henry Miller to Peter de Vries, the seducer (somewhat like Byron's Don Juan) becomes a victim of circumstances, a burlesque version of the knight-errant. Such writers tend to see, as did James Joyce in *Ulysses*, the whole business of sex as a cosmic joke. But most of the time, sex is taken seriously, indeed solemnly. Sex is self-expression; self-expression is freedom; freedom is good; hence sex is good. Hence, libertines and philanderers in infinite variety abound in our fiction, in every setting and on every social level, at cocktail parties and on commuter trains, in offices and slums, among Bohemians and philistines. Yet they never seem to have—indeed, they cannot have—the heroic or even semi-heroic dimensions of a Don Juan. Today, we are enlightened about sex; we like our fictional characters to defy convention, to be "adult" about having affairs in a we-know-what-we're-doing spirit. We understand such motives as loneliness, boredom, or genuine attraction; and above all, we allow them their Lawrencean ecstasies. But the philanderer as such, the man who moves from woman to woman, we regard as somehow sick.

And here we have Don Juan's ultimate predicament in the twentieth century—psychology. In other ages he could defy heaven, earth, the female spirit of the Great Goddess come back to rule; he cannot defy what amounts to the new puritanism of the unconscious. He could pull the beard of the Commander of Calatrava; he cannot, or has not yet learned, to pull Sigmund Freud's beard. He thrives on being called a villain, a damned soul; he can even stand ridicule; but he cannot stand the earnest admonition that he is immature, neurotic, compulsive.

There is an ironic paradox at work here. To begin with, psychoanalysis, by putting the sex instinct at the very center of life, seemed to promise to be Don Juan's ally. But this really proved a trap. If all men and women, and even the baby in the cradle, are Don Juans, where is his special daring? If his impulses are the result of a vague, scarcely understood force called the unconscious, what becomes of his rebellion? The classic Don Juan sins because he wills to; the psychological Don Juan acts because he cannot help himself. The only conceivable tragedy involving this kind of Don Juan is the tragedy of any man in the grip of an obsession or addiction that he cannot control: he is no more tragic than the alcoholic.

Yet the cult of psychoanalysis robs Don Juan even of this form of tragedy because it teaches that the addiction *can* be controlled, that with the help of analysis it can be cured like any illness. Freud tells Don Juan not that he must transcend his nature and become a model husband or a monk; it merely tells him that he should understand his "problem" as some form of neurosis and that he should limit the riot of his libido to reasonable proportions. He condemns Don Juan neither to damnation nor to a painful life of self-denial or self-struggle, but only to mediocrity.

In a sense, in America today, Don Juan has gone underground. His figure persists—in a rather hazy, misunderstood, marked-down form—in a kind of sub-literature never noticed by respectable critics: the tough-guy paperbacks and comics, semi-pornographic magazines, certain TV serials and movies. The men in all of these have two characteristics in common: they "take no nonsense" from women, and they more or less openly, if with a leer, praise sexual pleasure. Don Juan would not recognize himself in them, but he would at least recognize his hedonist side. Significantly, this libertine half-world—unlike the middle-brow, middle-class world of the American novel—is relatively uncowed by Freud. Part of Don Juan's fate in modern times, including this semi-underground status, is of course a specifically American or Anglo-Saxon phenomenon. In the Latin world he was always better understood and still retains a greater degree of reality. And yet the forces that war against Don Juan are not confined to any one culture and touch even his traditional Latin home: the decline of aristocracy, the new status of women, the weakening both of convention and of religion that leaves a rebel so much less to rebel against, the fading of the supernatural, and the cult of psychology, which makes excess no longer a sin but merely a disease, all spell Don Juan's end.

In Shaw's Man and Superman, *Don Juan,*
here played by Maurice Evans, is victim.

Don Juan's modern fate has been very aptly expressed in a minor but entertaining play entitled *The Death of Satan,* by the British playwright and poet Ronald Duncan, who has imagined what would happen if the legendary rake came back into the world today. Duncan's Don, possibly because of so many centuries in hell, has turned into more of a romantic than his classic model. For one thing, he spends his eternity of damnation pining for Doña Ana and writing her letters, in verse, that will never be delivered. Nevertheless, his return to earth is instructive: he rather recalls that other celebrated Don—Quixote—looking for knights to fight and for dragons to slay. Juan wants innocent maidens to seduce, jealous husbands to duel with, sins to commit—in effect, though Duncan doesn't say it that way, a God to defy. He finds none of these. When he sets out to make love to a married woman who is only too willing, the husband happens into the room and civilly offers Don Juan a drink.

When he finds Doña Ana, she has turned into a domineering modern career woman and a writer's fond, though scarcely passionate or faithful wife. Don Juan to her is now "obviously romantic and quite obviously immature." She is still woman enough to fall in love with him again—or something like love —and Don Juan is moved. But at the last moment he makes a discovery he cannot bear: the modern Ana does not believe in God. The cross she wears around her neck is a mere tourist's trinket. What the play is saying here is that Don Juan wanted nothing less than to be God's rival for Ana's love, in a sense to strike at Him through her. Since Ana no longer loves God, this is no longer possible, and before Don Juan flees back to hell in despair, he understands that—

If we don't love something greater than ourselves
We are incapable of loving one another. . . .
Now I see that He Who was between us
Was the One Who drew us together.
Now there is nothing between us, we are forever apart. . . .

You leave me nothing to look up to,
Nothing to overcome. Flesh of my flesh.
A man doesn't love his own flesh.
And the last twist of the knife is:
When a profligate atheist like me
Finds that the only thing he loves was the soul which he denied.

Henry Anatole Grunwald is a senior editor of Time. *He wrote "A Bernstein Suite" in the July, 1959, issue of* HORIZON.

65

After-Dark Satire Goes to Town

*Young cabaret rebels, "sick" comics,
far-out improvisers, are mounting a mass
assault on the idols of their audience*

A few moments after the curtain rose on *From the Second City,* a Chicago-born revue that opened in New York last fall, two men, Max and Moritz, appeared on stage and started to talk in abstract, scientific terms about experiments and possibilities. Their colloquy was succeeded by the sound of a piano playing the precise, rippling cadences of baroque music. To the accompaniment of the melody, Barbara Harris, a delectable blonde, came downstage and mimed a strip tease straight out of burlesque. First the imaginary gloves were removed and sailed into the auditorium. Next a scarf. Finally, accompanied by a series of sensual wriggles, the imaginary dress came reluctantly off. And Miss Harris slithered away, to all intents and purposes in undergarments.

"You see, Max?" said Moritz, reappearing. "I told you you could play Bach on Broadway and get away with it."

What you can also get away with, if they're good enough, is letting the actors make up their own jokes. This and the other sketches in *From the Second City* were invented by the cast itself, a practice that has been transferred to Broadway after creating a new boom in the cabaret business.

Cabarets now provide almost every kind of offbeat entertainment: poetry readings in bizarre coffeehouses from Boston to San Francisco's North Beach; studied shows with set scripts, elaborate music, and long runs at the "Medium Rare" in Chicago and at the "Upstairs at the Downstairs" in New York; high-priced folk singers at Chicago's "Gate of Horn"; jazz and blues and "sick" comics at the "Crystal Palace" in St. Louis; pantomime in New York's "Take 3"; new monologuists and new singers at "the hungry i" and "The Purple Onion" in San Francisco; traveling slapstick in a show called *Stewed Prunes*; and other variations at places with names like "Phase 2," "The Blind Pig," "Grecian Palace," "Versailles," and "Top Floor."

America's life and leisure, emblems and problems, arts and neuroses, excesses and successes, are uncovered and explored with pointed instruments by groups of young people who have learned to work comfortably together and who throw in a rehearsed or spontaneous gag at the moment they feel it will unstuff the greatest number of shirts. Sometimes the jokes are lifted from the day's news; more often they subvert the fads of an era: psychiatry and its practitioners are a popular target. In a sketch not long ago at the "Up-

stairs at the Downstairs" a young man who has been "working with my analyst on my virility anxiety," tells his girl friend that the analyst still hasn't given him permission to marry her. She wants to know why. "Don't ask me," he replies bitterly, "he's *your* father."

Out of intimate cabaret, a new generation of theater producers and comics has been born, including such "names" as Mike Nichols and Elaine May, Theodore J. (Ted) Flicker, Betty Comden and Adolph Green, Mort Sahl, Bob Newhart, Shelley Berman, Severn Darden, and Judy Holliday. Many of them have moved on to Broadway, off-Broadway, Hollywood, and other brightly lit places, as well as such dimly lit cells as night clubs and plush motels. The intimate cabaret has moved on, too, and become sharper, more polished, and sometimes more extemporaneous.

Today's cabaret has long roots that wind back to medieval court jesters, and perhaps even to Scheherazade, who talked through a thousand and one nights to save her skin. But its present pattern comes more directly from the free-swinging revues of London, Paris, Munich, and Berlin, from American vaudeville skits and burlesque by-play, and from a group of young theater rebels in Chicago who felt that there was not enough give and take between performers and audiences in slick Broadway-type shows.

The chief rebel was—and is—the young man who last fall directed the Broadway production of *From the Second City,* and who has restored an appreciable amount of topical humor and satire to the national entertainment scene. He is Paul Sills, a squat, medium-sized man who knows what he wants and whose secret is that he is inexhaustible.

As a very young man he knew that he wanted his own theater. He was acting at the University of Chicago Theater at the time, gradually giving up the idea of pursuing an academic career any further. With David Shepherd, a restless Harvard graduate who visited Chicago and wanted to start *his* own theater, Sills opened one that year, using actors recruited from the University, on the second floor of a small and battered building on the Near North Side.

Their Playwrights company produced everything from Shakespeare and Ibsen and Strindberg to Chekhov and Sartre and Shaw, presenting plays Chicago would not otherwise have seen, such as *Wozzeck* and *The Caucasian Chalk Circle.* Local critics and audiences supported them, and Sills

By H. E. F. DONOHUE

The Second City. *Top left: Paul Sills and David Shepherd, fathers of this Chicago-based venture in spontaneous satirical cabaret, discuss a scene during the early days of their theater partnership. Top right: In their recent New York production a take-off on Sir Edmund Hillary's Himalayan adventures finds two mountaineers (actors Andrew Duncan, left, and Paul Sand, right) surveying the snowscape while holding an imaginary rope attached to a third climber, who is being clutched by a bear. Center: Garry Sherman, the show's pianist, conducts "The Second City Symphony," a mock orchestral recital of the work of the company's resident composer, William Mathieu; performers include, from left, the actors Howard Alk (guitar), Mina Kolb (little bells), Paul Sand (tin whistle), Eugene Troobnick (horn), Barbara Harris (clarinet), Andrew Duncan (trombone), and Severn Darden (cymbal). Below left: Mocking a strip tease, Barbara Harris throws a come-up-and-see-me look at the customers. Right: Paul Sand and some disembodied hands improvise on a scene that travesties a nightmarish Ingmar Bergman movie.*

PHOTOGRAPHED BY MORTON SHAPIRO

and Shepherd moved to a larger hall and built a better stage —concerned, however, as to whether or not they might be "selling out" to success.

For these young men were dismayed both by the state of the world and the state of the theater. Threats to individual freedom, particularly as personified by the junior Senator from Wisconsin, then approaching his zenith, aroused them. Commercial theater, they thought, together with slick movies and that monster of mediocrity, television, was leading the way toward a static, conformist American society. Merely to maintain a theater for the affluent, merely to amuse with other men's work seemed not enough. Both of them wanted to comment directly on current events. Both thought, along with Captain Jack Boyle of O'Casey's *Juno and the Paycock,* that "th' whole worl's in a terrible state o' chassis." The only thing a sensible man could do was to laugh. "We should run a small bar," Shepherd would say. "A workingmen's bar. Ask *them* for ideas, and act them out on the spot."

After two years they closed down their successful little theater, rented a bar, recruited players from the old company, and opened a cabaret based on improvisations, which they called "The Compass." Their house was not a workingmen's bar but a small place near the University of Chicago, and their audience was made up of the people you might expect to see around a university.

In planning "The Compass," Sills recalled something he had done as a member of a children's acting group which had been directed by his mother. They had toured grammar schools in the 1930's—"doing anything," he says, "and everything. We put on little plays from ideas that the kids in the audience shouted out. We were amazing. And very funny." Sills later used some of the same "imprahv" (improvisational) techniques in directing the Playwrights company. Most trained actors know the form; many use "imprahvs" to warm up. One of Sills's exercises had the actors run through an intricate plot using only nonsense dialogue; another had individual actors move through a stage crowded with imaginary objects and furniture.

The results had amused him, particularly during the rehearsals of Mike Nichols and Elaine May, two of the company's most adept improvisers. Both Sills and Shepherd held in high esteem history's first extemporizers: the artist-clowns of the *commedia dell' arte.* This great technique of spontaneity in the theater—beginning in the middle of the seventeenth century in Italy, and later in France—had established a bold tradition. It had also proved that a small group of actors—from three to six in number—holding nothing sacred and obeying only the law that the audience must be made to laugh, could work the whole range of human fate and foible without the aid of props, scenery, costumes, or scripts.

In America improvisation persisted in vaudeville skits and in the work of the burlesque comics. After World War II colorful bits of satire tentatively lifted their heads like crocuses through the snow. Comden and Green and a girl named Judy Holliday did skits at the Village Vanguard in New York, "taking off" now and then to ad-lib about current events. In the early 1950's Julius Monk made it fash-

ionable to sit in his small cabaret, the "Upstairs at the Downstairs," for the express purpose of *not* getting drunk, but rather to regard the efforts of bright young entertainers as they cleverly executed set pieces, much like a Renaissance masque for the court elite.

In San Francisco at "the hungry i," a young and eternally postcollegiate man named Mort Sahl was obliquely heckling every public figure in sight, his own generation, and himself, affecting in his monologues the intellectual stance of the cultural anthropology student who drives a sports car: stunned and bemused, but unalienated. Bob Newhart, the button-down comedian, was still entertaining friends, buffing his delivery. In New York a group of students at the Actors' Studio who were embellishing an improvised scene about a dope addict, caught the attention of a writer named Michael V. Gazzo, and they all wound up composing a play (later adapted into a movie) called *A Hatful of Rain.*

But it remained for Sills and Shepherd to bring improvisational technique to its full flower. For their "Compass" shows they started with scenes worked out in rough outline before opening night. While the show was in progress, the actors called for suggestions from the audience (a first and last line, situations, styles)—the so-called "true" imprahvs, which developed during the performance. But even the practiced pieces had begun as improvisations, in response to a news headline or to someone's fantastic idea, with Sills watching and stopping the actors when he felt they were going the wrong way, that is, becoming dull, un-funny, or merely progressing toward a clownish cliché.

Nichols and May later brought some of these scenes to television on the Jack Paar and Ed Sullivan shows, with, of course, variations. The famous teen-age love scene in the back of the automobile is one example. The girl is worried about "respect"; the boy is just worried. "Believe me," he tells her, before they finally embrace, "I will have nothing *but* respect for you." In another vignette, the two play a noisy disc jockey and his overly co-operative starlet guest:

He: "Tell me baby, what do you think of Albert Schweitzer?"

She: "Well, I am sure he is a terribly nice fellow, although I myself have never been out with him."

One of the "Compass" group's early comments on scientific secrecy involved a young scientist trying to copyright the results of ten years' research. He is told that not only has the same work been completed five years before by another, it has been marked top secret and is still unpublishable. The crushed young man then asks for his manuscript back but cannot have it: it, too, is now classified.

The "Compass" became a solid hit with Chicago audiences. People who wandered by could sneak a look through the front window of the modest theater. If they were attracted inside, a beer would buy them an evening's entertainment. The content of the shows changed from week to week. In addition to the "polished imprahvs" and suggestions from the audience, the performers might do a ten-second spot in the individual style of some literary figure. For Erskine Caldwell they would go into a tight lovers' clinch until the girl broke loose with: "Bye, daddy, see you after school." A

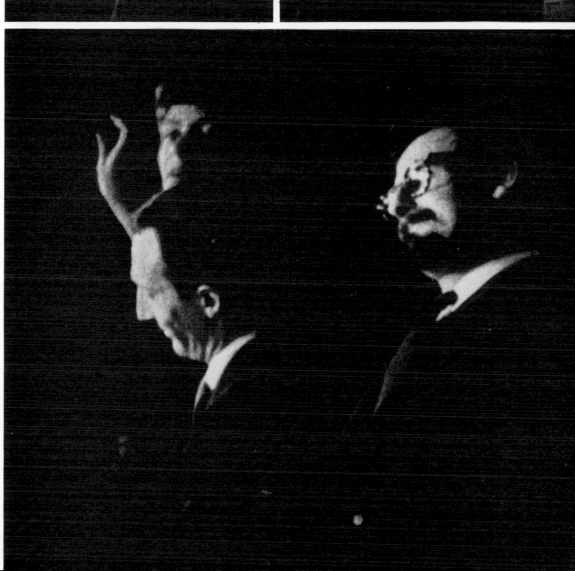

The Premise. *Top: Ted Flicker, the guiding spirit and chief performer of this intimate cabaret on Bleecker Street in downtown New York, submits to having his nose tweaked. The scene is a skit on David Susskind's TV interview in 1960 with Khrushchev, in which Mr. K (left) humbles his host (Flicker) for asking impudent questions. Left center: Joan Darling and Jim Frawley parody a romantic encounter between two teen-agers. (In the sketch preceding this, Miss Darling plays a nun who has just won a Mississippi river boat in a dice game.) Right center: Exuberant critical notices decorate the entrance to "The Premise," whose patrons sit in a long, narrow, dark hall, with exotic coffees and pastry perched on their armrests as they watch the proceedings. Below: Tom Aldredge (left) and Flicker (right), introduced by Miss Darling, are puppets who speak for the cities of Algiers and Bizerte, and are seated on the knees of a third actor, Frawley (out of sight), who represents General de Gaulle. At the end of the sketch the "puppets" run off into the darkness, carrying their "master."*

character out of Françoise Sagan would tell his soul mate: "This has been the most sordid, dirty, vulgar affair of my life." Her reply: "Don't say another word. You'll spoil it."

Two companies sprang from the "Compass" beginnings. One went to St. Louis under the direction of Ted Flicker, a large, comfortably padded epicure with a trim beard, a two-tone, second-hand Bentley, and financial backing; this group opened "The Compass Players" in the "Crystal Palace" and played to packed houses for nine months. The other group stayed in Chicago under Sills's direction and opened a theater called "The Second City." Next door to it they built a new theater, again called "Playwrights," where they produced first *The Explainers,* a musical revue based on the book by Jules Feiffer, and then a modern version of *The Beggar's Opera,* set in Chicago and called *The Big Deal,* with all but the songs improvised.

The two groups eventually reached New York, with separate productions off and on Broadway respectively, although Flicker's team, functioning as "The Premise" on Bleecker Street, has been modified. Sooner or later Flicker plans to "rotate Premise companies" across the country. Sills's company landed in the Royale Theatre on Broadway with its *From the Second City* intact. The New York reviewers derived much pleasure and quotable material from the revue. Both groups are still supposedly improvising, although it is doubtful whether more than a small proportion of the shows is completely unrehearsed. Much of the material seems to have been preconceived and pieced together, when the time came, to fit requests of the audience.

The principal difference between Flicker's and Sills's shows comes from the difference in temperament and intention between the two men. Sills often seems sour and churlish, a barker of commands who will suddenly lapse into muttering through clenched teeth. Then, at the mention or thought of something droll or outrageous, his sad, round face melts into a young man's smile: pensive and pleased. The smile may disappear just as suddenly. Sills likes to assault an audience with his material, to jab them, startle them, sometimes to sadden them.

In a typical *Second City* sketch an American commentator talks to a German youth about the neo-Nazi movement in West Germany. The youth denies its existence but admits that he belongs to a new group, an anti-Nazi *Bund.* "We have armbands, see?" He shows his armband to the audience. "See? My armband!" He turns back to the commentator. "And we have uniforms, and we march." The commentator then wants to know what is the aim of the new *Bund.* The youth answers: "The final solution of the Nazi problem."

Now, these lines happen to be the ones delivered during a particular performance. They may be quite different the following night. The same goes for another scene in which, on one night, a Southern governor tells an interviewer: "It will be slow. We are in a difficult transitional period now . . . until we can return to segregation."

Flicker's scenes at "The Premise" are less ferocious. He wins the audience over, enlists them, and makes them feel they are part of the attack, not its target. His resident com-

pany did not, at first, intend to do much political satire. "It was the audience that demanded it when we asked for ideas," Flicker says, "so we had to begin working things up."

Southern governors have appeared in "The Premise" routines, too. One of them is making a harangue when, in the middle of a sentence, he has a heart attack, drops dead, and goes to Heaven. There he meets God and explains who he is. God responds: "Is that so? Well, I'se de Lawd."

A rash of coffeehouse cabarets has spread across Greenwich Village in the last few years. A young impresario named David Gordon opened the first so-called theater café, "Phase 2," which used written sketches and songs. Gordon's *New Phases of 1960* unleashed a number of new writers, some of whom later worked for Julius Monk in his uptown "Upstairs." Somewhere between the written *New Phases of 1960* and the unwritten shows of "The Premise," another kind of show, *Stewed Prunes,* served itself up at an establishment called "Take 3."

The cult of new, intimate, fairly vicious, semi-improvised satire, then, is taking hold fast. But how good is it? The standards of any one show seem to vary widely from night to night. "It all depends," says one actor, "on how we feel and on the quality of the audience."

For, after all, the audience comes to a cabaret of this type in order to subject itself to the players and to see its own image reflected in a distorted—or possibly not so distorted—shape. The man who makes ugly faces at himself in a mirror is not necessarily a work of art, nor even of passing interest. If, to have great clowns, we must have great audiences, then we seem to have both. Moreover, with spontaneity that either is or at least *seems* improvised, the theater has found a new kind of frankness—one that allows us to bear up under the scrutiny of the clown inside ourselves.

One of the liveliest scenes in *Second City* comes toward the close of the evening. It is the end of the world, and all the animals are being welcomed into the ark by Noah. He asks the animals in turn what their individual roles or "functions" are; in other words, what have they done—what can they do—to be saved? One actor, playing an aardvark, sadly admits he has no function. Noah suggests that he might eat ants. The idea repels him. Says Noah: "Eat a few at a picnic once in a while. Who'll know?"

The ark sails, leaving one animal, the centaur, ashore. Moments later, his wife appears, apologizing for her late arrival; she had to finish locking the house. When she learns that the ark has gone, she says—it is an instant of tenderness—"And you waited for me?" The rain begins, and she puts up an umbrella. He asks, "Is there room for me under the umbrella?" And they stand, two centaurs, sheltering together, watching the ark draw away across the waters.

On this, the show ends—except for a song, in the course of which the whole company sings to the audience, "There won't be water, but *fire* next time."

H. E. F. Donohue, whose articles and stories have appeared in many magazines, acted and directed at the University of Chicago Theater, at a time when some of today's leading "instant" cabaret performers started their careers there.

Upstairs at the Downstairs. *On New York's West Fifty-sixth Street Julius Monk's young company is dedicated to the late-evening lampoon. Above: Bill McCutcheon sings that he would rather be an amoeba than a man—for then, if an H-bomb fell, he'd split into several amoebas and swim happily ever after through the slime. Right: In a spoof on D. H. Lawrence's novel, Jim Sheridan as the gamekeeper teaches Lovelady Powell as Lady Chatterley to use hard, four-letter words—"dirt" instead of "earth," "wash" instead of "freshen up." The show is* Dressed to the Nines.

Phase 2. *Not far from "The Premise" a sign (near right) heralds another New York cabaret on Bleecker Street. Far right: One of the show's principals, Judy Martin, sings a tribute to her "Town of Romance"—Secaucus, the meat-packing metropolis of New Jersey. Below: The entire company (of four) tells how "You, Too, Can Belong" to a Greenwich Village "in-group" by buying a beatnik package—tattered sweater, jeans, and a less-than-kempt beard. Singers are, from left, Lucienne Bridou, Bill Heyer, Judy Martin, Larry Hankin. Heyer, who wrote the show, called it* The Heyer Things of Life.

CAVE-DWELLING CARVERS OF 5,000 YEARS AGO

A troglodyte culture in the Negev yields a trove of ivory figurines

By JEAN PERROT

An aerial view of the excavated area at Safadi shows the underground chambers of the troglodyte settlement of 3500 B.C. The tunnels (right) often reached a depth of 23 feet. From the workshop of a cave-dwelling carver comes the woman's head in ivory (opposite page), with appropriately big, staring eyes, and holes cut in the skull for the purpose of stringing the piece as a pendant.

Fifteen centuries before Abraham settled in Beersheba and five hundred years before the Pyramid Age in Egypt, a foreign population entered Palestine from the northeast. These pastoral people, who probably came from the steppes bordering the Syro-Arabian desert, became the first dwellers in the Negev, the southern, semiarid region of Israel. Their remarkable settlements, dating back more than 5,000 years, have been uncovered by recent excavations at Safadi and Abu Matar, near Beersheba.

The villages constructed by this people were entirely subterranean. They are composed of extensive caves dug straight down into the alluvial soil on the banks of the wadi, or dry river-bed. The discovery of this troglodyte way of life could finally explain the cave-dwelling Horites whom Biblical scholars were always surprised to find mentioned as living in this caveless part of the country.

Such a subterranean settlement offers protection from the searing heat of the day, the chill of the night, and the biting wind-borne sands of the desert. It seems less likely that security from enemy tribes was the reason for building underground, since the absence of weapons or fortifications reflects rather a life of peace centered around trade and agriculture.

Distributed around a central communal hall

TEXT CONTINUED ON PAGE 74

PHOTOGRAPHS ARIE VOLK

TEXT CONTINUED FROM PAGE 73

and admirably preserved to this day, the underground dwellings were found complete with their furnishings: decorated pottery, basalt basins and pedestaled bowls, ornaments, bracelets, necklaces, bone and ivory objects. Copper tools, the oldest yet found in Israel, were made on the spot by casting. Since copper ores are not found in the immediate vicinity, the evidence of a copper industry at Beersheba suggests commercial relations before 3000 B.C. with the Jordanian plateau, a source of copper ore, basalt, and other hard stones, or even with the metallurgical centers of the Caucasus.

The most remarkable finds are the ivory figurines. The local production of these objects was established by the discovery of an ivory carver's workshop, complete with tools, a workbench, and the raw material—an elephant tusk. Although elephants are known to have existed in Syria, it is also possible that an active ivory trade was carried on with Africa, down the channel of the Red Sea.

These statuettes, found in the dwellings, may represent worshipers standing in ritual nakedness before a divinity, or may be connected with some magical or other religious practices. They bear some resemblance to pre-Dynastic Egyptian figurines, but are superior in the delicacy of conception and vigor of execution. The simplicity of execution produces a certain stiffness in general attitude but vitality is not absent, and the sensitiveness of the artist to the grace of the female body is clearly evident in the figure of the pregnant woman. Unrelated to any previously known school in the Middle East, the Beersheba figurines provide the first glimpse of an amazingly early and original school of art.

Jean Perrot, head of the French Archaeological Mission in Israel, directed the Beersheba excavations which uncovered the Safadi caves.

Probably connected to a fertility cult was the statuette (far left) of a pregnant woman with an exaggerated navel. The male figure (above left) wearing an incised "Libyan sheath" over the genitals was found (below) in a cache with other objects. The holes in the head and cheeks of the male head (below left) were for inserting tufts of hair. Other pieces include an ivory pin in stylized bird shape and a woman's head with hair swirled in a bun supporting an animal headdress.

Floating Rocks and Flaming Tubas

René Magritte, whose *Castle of the Pyrenees* floats so miraculously on the facing page, is a Belgian artist who, at sixty-three, is a contender for the title of the leading fantasist painter today. By classification Magritte is a surrealist, and he was a member of the wedding that mated horseplay with intellectualism to establish the movement. Surrealism has become our century's official version of man's spottily continuous exploration of the world of dream and necromancy, but even as a certified surrealist, Magritte has always remained a little apart from the organization in a way that is refreshing. And the fact that the word "refreshing" can be used in connection with him is the first indication of the difference between Magritte and his colleagues.

As a surrealist painting, *Castle of the Pyrenees* follows rule number one of the surreal formula: it combines familiar things painted in acutely recognizable detail, but combines them in irrational relationships. The elements composing the picture are trite enough—the lovely blue sky feathered with fluffy white clouds, the sea with its breakers, the fortified castle picturesquely situated on a huge rock. (Or is it a tiny rock hugely painted? This is a typical Magritte disconcerter.) Everything is trite—except that the rock floats,

which is certainly the least trite thing that a rock can do.

So much for the formula, which is one that any painter skilled in the technique of realistic painting and possessed of any feeling for paradox can apply in reasonable expectation of arresting our attention. But just why *Castle of the Pyrenees* is as effective as it is, and why it not only arrests our attention but then holds it, and during continued acquaintance impresses us less and less with its novelty and more and more with its mystery, is more difficult to say.

Like any other painter whose true art begins where his mastery of the brush leaves off, Magritte has his own sensitivities to scale, color, arrangement, and the other factors that go to make up a picture, and his own ways of adjusting them to produce the picture he wants—ways that he probably could not explain but whose right or wrong use he can detect as he plans and paints. One bit of this picture, however, that might not be noticed is demonstrably and typically Magritte: the sly use of a banal technique in the painting of the sea and breakers.

This seascape is wonderfully routine. Another fantasist might have yielded to the temptation to give the water a magically glassy smoothness or the waves a fantastic char-

René Magritte: Castle of the Pyrenees, *1955*

Hieronymus Bosch: Temptation of St. Anthony, *detail*

The first, and still the most mysterious, of the great Flemish fantasists was Bosch (left). His demons exist on a level of imagination altogether different from the heavy-handed literalism of Wiertz's too-hasty burial (below), or from Ensor's skeletons wrangling over a hanged man (right). Closer to Bosch in spirit are the haunted faces of the contemporary Landuyt (far right).

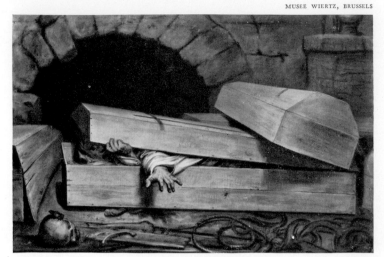

Antoine Wiertz: Precipitate burial, *1854*

acter in an effort to fortify the effect of total enchantment. But Magritte, who knows exactly where and when to gild a lily, chose not only to paint an ordinary sea but to paint it in an ordinary way, the way any routine hack seascapist would have done.

No other treatment could have so potently forced us to accept the reality of the impossibly floating rock. This single irreality is so perfectly integrated with familiar realities that we must accept it, or deny them. We cannot redirect our entire acquaintance with the physical world by denying those familiar clouds, that blue sky, that rocky texture, that tourist-delight Carcassonnesque castle, the consistency of the light. Above all, we cannot deny that sea, which is doubly ordinary as an ordinary sea painted in an ordinary way. And the rock comes with it.

Magritte's power as a fantasist is not so much that he presents us with the fantastic as something unexplainable, as that he presents it to us as something unquestioned. A fantasist of Salvador Dali's ilk offers us a conglomeration of impossibilities, which partially convince simply because they are presented in acute detail. A Dali *Castle of the Pyrenees* could be expected to include a dozen or two dozen fantastic

elements, such as flaming giraffes emerging from the glassy water, limp watches draped on the castle walls, rotting monsters on the beach—a beach, by the way, that Magritte is canny enough to omit, thus giving added solidity to the castled rock by leaving it the one solid, nonfluid element in the picture.

Dali takes us into madhouses where we remain sane observers, or, say, to a cocktail party of freaks where our normalcy may make us feel out of place but does not lead us to question it as the standard from which the rest of the company departs. But in a picture like *Castle of the Pyrenees* Magritte takes us to a party where all the guests are normal but one. This one is a person who, while otherwise normal, floats around the ceiling like an escaped balloon. This floating, however, is unquestioned; the other guests obviously accept it as nothing extraordinary. To point out the abnormality would be rude at best and dangerous at worst, since we begin to wonder why we, alone, find the circumstance unusual. The end is that we begin not to doubt our own eyes but to doubt our experience, which has taught us that people do not float. We are taken into the world of the fantastic as a participant rather than as a spectator. By his

James Ensor: Skeletons arguing over a corpse, *1891*

Octave Landuyt: Petrifaction, *1960*

matter-of-factness and by a kind of pictorial understate-ment—an economy in the use of fantastic elements com-bined with commonplace ones—Magritte seduces us into the act, while Dali merely performs for us as we watch.

Magritte's being a Belgian impresses some people as a fact at least as contradictory as the contradictions upon which his art rests. "Belgium" is not a word that conjures up first of all a vision of fantasy. The country's hybrid tra-dition, part French and part Flemish, suggests rather the offspring of a parentage in which practical values are genetic dominants that have crowded out more lightsome recessives. French delicacy, the nuance of taste and intellect, the vi-vacity that is part of the Latin heritage in the French com-pound, and all the other parts of the compound that have always tempered and enlarged French practicality, we think of as having got lost somewhere north of the Franco-Belgian border. Brussels may be called the second Paris, but it is a Paris where, from cuisine and show girls to the monetary system and politics, everything is somehow a heavier, steadier, less imaginative proposition. Nevertheless Belgian art includes recurrent appearances of fantasy that are not paralleled by French art in its most *outré* expressions.

The Flemish half of the Belgian inheritance is another story, although here also one is likely to associate Belgium first with the solid, practical Dutch tradition of the Low Countries. Flemish art of the late Middle Ages, the glory of the country's artistic achievement, was an art of realistic vo-cabulary in which the visible world received explicit examina-tion and detailed restatement. But among these painters there is hardly one, from Van Eyck on, who did not also di-rect his realism toward mystical statement or toward diable-rie, with Hieronymus Bosch cropping up among them as the world's acknowledged genius of the fantastic.

Scholars point out that Bosch's marvelously grotesque and terrifying art (see page 78) was inspired as much by treatises of the day as by personal vision. And his successor, Pieter Bruegel the Elder, was more interested in examining man's nature and his behavior as a social animal than he was in the apparent fantasies in which he couched his con-clusions. But any tradition that includes these two names must be conceded a dominating position in the history of fantasy even though its expression, as fantasy in painting has a way of doing, fades out and then recurs only upon stimulation by new impulses.

79

Although both of these paintings are fairly inscrutable, they do show one difference between the fifteenth and twentieth centuries. The lady in the anonymous Sortilège d'amour *(right) is clearly mistress of her fate: she is preparing some sort of love philter. But the one in Paul Delvaux's* La Prisonnière *(opposite) can only wander helplessly —or is she sleepwalking?—through the moonlit colonnades of an empty imaginary Roman forum.*

The impulses were especially strong during the nineteenth century and on into the twentieth. Upon its wilder shores, nineteenth-century romanticism tossed up the Belgian Antoine Wiertz (see page 78) as one of its most bizarre figures. Born in 1806, Wiertz died in 1865, and during that span he managed to reflect Victor Hugo, Rubens, Gustave Doré, the entire school of German romantic painters, Michelangelo, certain baroque Italians, the worst of Landseer, a bit of Poussinesque classicism, some bastard Raphaelesque sentiment, and much genuine bourgeois sentimentalism, in paintings depicting murders, visions of death, revolts in hell, rapes, witches performing the black mass, the Triumph of Christ, the Deposition of Christ, alluring nude-bosomed pneumatic virgins leaning out of their frames to offer the observer a symbolic rosebud, dogs guarding their mistresses' bonnets, carnivals, promenades, portraits, and subjects from classical history, either idyllic or tempestuous.

Among his many gods, Wiertz was most passionately attached to his countryman Rubens, whose voluptuous grandeur he managed to reduce to a kind of fatty fury. He left the mass of his paintings for eternity in a riotous and wonderful house of horrors, the Musée Wiertz in Brussels, where

one of the pictures (as an indication of the general character of the place) is installed to be seen through a keyhole. And yet Wiertz, for all his atrocious, ill-digested eclecticism, for all the awkwardness of his synthetic literary and painterly allusions to disharmonious sources, is a fantasist of insane power, even if, like so much insanity, he manifests its genuineness in forms of absurdity. In any history of Belgian art, romantic art, or fantastic art, Wiertz deserves a special, if not altogether enviable, place.

Like many fantasists, Wiertz was essentially naïve in spirit. His trouble was that his naïveté was at odds with his technique, which was academically proficient in the manner of his day. Give him a fresher, more individual way of painting and he would be seen to be more closely related to the currently admired Belgian fantasist James Ensor than is generally recognized.

Ensor was born in 1860, five years before Wiertz's death, and lived until 1949. He has become important as a precursor of expressionism, but he is fully his own man only when we regard him as an independent visionary. Like Wiertz, he was concerned with bacchanals of death and deceit; his two recurrent spooky symbols are the skeleton and

the mask, representing man's mortality and his falsity (see page 79). Unlike Wiertz, Ensor had the good fortune to resist, or to be incapable of absorbing and holding, the teaching to which he was subjected at the Brussels Academy; he developed instead the personal style that gave his ponderings on violence and injustice (which were also Wiertz's ponderings) the character of private fantasies rather than social documents.

There is no reason why problems of violence and injustice cannot be expressed in an academic style, but when the ponderer is, like Ensor, an eccentric recluse, a conventional and public style is inappropriate, as it proved to be for poor Wiertz. We are always aware, in front of a painting by Ensor, that this is not a skilled painter in conventional terms and not a sound and reasonable thinker in the broadest scope of social problems. But he is a beautiful painter in a way all his own, and if he is naïve intellectually, he is rich emotionally. Whatever he set out to say in broad social terms, he managed to say only in such specialized and eccentric ones that he emerges, willy-nilly, as a fantasist.

The Belgian generation following Ensor includes not only Magritte but also Paul Delvaux as members of the first organized movement of fantasists. Artists of fantasy are ordinarily individuals whose private worlds make them so; almost by definition a fantasist is not part of a group. But surrealism was, of course, a movement with a literary manifesto, a program, and a built-in public relations department with a policy based on shock values. Delvaux is much closer than Magritte to the surreal norm; for one thing, he is conspicuously engaged in the Freudian, semi-Freudian, or pseudo-Freudian sexualities that are uppermost in the public personality of the movement. Not that Magritte has not turned out some jobs of this kind—and some honeys—but he has tended to work away from rather than deeper into such themes. Delvaux, on the other hand, is a painter so sexual as to be embarrassing upon occasion. His nudes, although young and of proportions that should be adequately attractive, have the anti-allure of individuals stripped for medical attention and probably in need of it.

The similarity between the *Sortilège d'amour* by an unknown fifteenth-century Flemish master and Delvaux's *La Prisonnière* (both reproduced above) is probably a coincidence, but a fortunate one for purposes of contrasting programmatic fantasies five centuries apart. The *Sortilège* is an allegory, in which a good iconographer could identify each element as a standard symbolical accessory to the subject (the dog for fidelity, the various flowers representing other virtues or attributes, and so on). The apparent fantasy is a by-product of allegory. In much contemporary surrealism, fantasy can be translated in terms of the Freudian dream book, but the symbolism, if it can be called that, is informal. It can come from the painter's own subconscious, his unconscious, or his quite conscious intention to startle us.

Magritte's fantasies also can be subjected to Freudian analysis, since there is almost nothing that cannot be, even when fantasy is not involved. *Night at Pisa,* for instance, involving a tower and a spoon (page 86), supplies pat elementary symbols for any amateur psychiatrist. But to play this game with Magritte is to make mere charades, essentially literary charades, of paintings that have admirably little dependence upon literary associations. The trouble with much surrealism is that it goes over the edge that divides the art of painting from the art of literature—becomes, in short, illustration, thus losing its independence as a purely visual art. Magritte usually avoids this error, although he takes us out of this world into an eerie one just as a teller of fantastic tales may do.

But he takes us out of this world, not by narrating an incident, but by dissolving the concepts of time and space and volume and tangible relatives upon which our experience of this world is based. *Night at Pisa* sounds explicit enough, and an explicit list could be made of the elements that compose it. But it is totally unexplicit on the scores that attach us to this world and account for whatever security we may feel within it. Is the tower normal-sized and the spoon huge, or the spoon normal and the tower dwarfed? More than being either, they are neither. We do not really know what the size of things is, and as a result we do not really know what size we are. And in *The Personal Values* (page 84) we cannot say that the room, the armoire, and the bed are full-sized, and the comb, the goblet, the shaving brush, soap, and match are of gigantic proportions, or the reverse. Could we pick up this goblet from within the tiny model of a room; or standing in this room, would we be looking up at the bowl of the goblet from our full height below it? The sensation of lost scale must be akin to that of weightlessness; within a Magritte we are as far removed from this world as is the man in the spaceship.

Magritte's manipulation of scale is his most explicable device, although the subtleties of his control remain unaccountable, just as we can point out but not entirely explain the effectiveness of his denial of materiality by giving one substance, a rock, the property of another, a gas. And in any case these elements in Magritte's art, basic as they are, are shared by other surrealists.

What separates Magritte, in the end, from other surrealists is that the pretentious morbidities upon which the school has too often fed, and which finally become so wearisome, have never dominated his themes and have flavored them less and less in his late work. Never pretentious, Magritte is sometimes content to be merely delightfully witty, as in *The Plagiarism* (page 85), where a spring landscape is revealed in a cutout shape of a bouquet of flowers. With a similar device more disturbingly used, he throws us off balance in *The Human Condition II* (page 87) by dissolving a canvas to reveal the scene behind it—or something. The titles may or may not mean anything, just as the titles of *The Rights of Man* (page 83) or of *Secrets of the Horizon* and *The Unexpected Answer* (page 86) are not explanations of what is going on, but gentle shoves to make us wonder about things in our own way. Magritte never tells a story; he is a painter of absolutely concrete impossibilities that play on thousands of associations. His genius is that he enchants the eye as an entrance to the mind, which he equally delights and disconcerts.

In a new Belgian generation, Octave Landuyt, now thirty-nine, is a fantasist unlike Magritte and even more in the indigenous tradition. Magritte's quality of delectation and his wit attach him to French traditions. Landuyt is a Fleming who knows his Bosch and obviously reveres without imitating him. Still maturing as an artist, Landuyt sometimes paints huge grotesque and disturbing heads like *Petrifaction* (page 79), in which some critics find overtones of social protest or humanistic compassion; sometimes huge imagined insects; and most recently, large canvases that he calls "essential surfaces," in which animal, vegetable, and mineral forms seem to be examined under a microscope.

Coral, bark, and diseased livers are suggested by some of them, and like Bosch, Landuyt paints his disturbing subjects in colors of the most glowing beauty. Octave Landuyt is the latest indication that Belgium's double tradition is more and more persistently bringing out, rather than pushing back, the genetic recessive of the fantastic.

On the following five pages:

A portfolio of

paintings by René Magritte.

Opposite: The Rights of Man, *1948*

The Personal Values, *1952*

The Plagiarism, *1945*

Night at Pisa, *1952*

The Unexpected Answer, *1933*

The Secrets of the Horizon, *1955*

Opposite: The Human Condition II, *1935*

"Perhaps many of the complaints about my manner on the stage are justified—but if I am a little bit more obtrusive than some, it is because I am in some kind of intense relationship to what is going on"

Glenn Gould

An interview by BERNARD ASBELL

In the young but much-chronicled career of Glenn Gould, reviewers while praising his pianistic wizardry have been equally fascinated by his personal eccentricities: his insistence upon overheated rooms; his predilection for wearing mittens and two sets of sweaters indoors; his supposed horror of drafts, of tobacco smoke, and of shaking hands. So when I approached his hotel suite near New York's Central Park, I could not say that I hadn't been warned as to what I might encounter.

When the door opened I experienced a mild shock. My host's long, youthful face was lit by unrestrained friendliness, and he hailed me right in. He was in shirt sleeves—no sweaters at all. The room itself was not uncomfortably warm. True, his hair flopped in long blond strands along the sides of his head, and he was wearing no shoes.

I asked if he objected to the use of a tape recorder. He didn't at all. He only wanted the microphone placed at the level of his face, explaining that for reasons he could never understand, he is uncomfortable addressing anything low. (At the piano, he sits in an uncommonly low chair, the keyboard almost at his chin, which has caused him to suffer a certain amount of critical ridicule.)

He sank deeply into a sofa, reached for the telephone, called room service, and ordered two pots of coffee. (I had heard that he never drank anything but Poland Water.) He didn't even mind my lighting a cigarette.

I decided then and there, perhaps on insufficient evidence, that although he might have minor oddities, Glenn Gould was not the freak that some writers had made him out to be. His oddities would hardly draw a second glance if he were not, at the age of twenty-nine, one of the most astonishing pianists in the memory of man.

Gould began to play the piano at the age of three. Before he could read words, his mother, an amateur pianist, had taught him to read notes in their home in Toronto. Ten years later, after substituting professional instruction for his mother's, he was recognized as the best boy musician in Canada. In another six years he was through with teachers. "I decided," he has said, "it was time to set out on my own snowshoes, and I developed an insufferable amount of self-confidence, which has never left me."

In preparing for my interview, I read the notes Gould had written for the backs of his record albums. They are good warm-ups for conversation with him. Here is a typical example from the notes to his album of Bach's *Goldberg Variations:*

"The most casual acquaintance with this work—a first hearing, or a brief glance at the score—will manifest the baffling incongruity between the impossible dimensions of the variations and the unassuming *Sarabands* which conceived them. . . . We are dealing with possibly the most brilliant substantiation of a ground bass in history, for in my opinion, the fundamental variative ambition of this work is not to be found in organic fabrication but in a community of sentiment. . . ."

After this, conversation with him was a snap.

INTERVIEWER: When did you decide to make a career of playing the piano?

GOULD: I think I was truly determined upon a career in music at the age of nine or ten. I was determined to wrap myself up in music because I found it was a damned good way of avoiding my schoolmates, with whom I did not get along. I was not a prodigy, at least not an exploited one. I didn't do any concerts, except playing perhaps at a church social, but I wrote my own little masterpieces. I don't think I really began to accept myself as a serious professional threat until I was twenty and actually earning a living playing the piano in radio and television studios. I was still in school at this point, but I began to realize that it was possible, albeit with considerable effort, to make this thing practical. The form of achievement I imagined, however, didn't really involve my playing the piano.

Another in the HORIZON interview series
THE ARTIST SPEAKS FOR HIMSELF

Throughout my teens I rather resisted the idea of a career as a concert pianist.

INTERVIEWER: Resisted?

GOULD: Yes, it seemed like a kind of superficial thing, some sort of pleasant adjunct to a scholastic interest in music, you know. I imagined that only a career that was musicologically motivated was worthy and that everything else was a little bit frivolous. I saw myself as a sort of musical Renaissance Man, capable of doing many things. I obviously wanted to be a composer. I still do. Performing in the arena had no attraction for me. This was, at least in part, defensive. Even from what little I then knew of the politics of the business, it was apparent that a career as a solo pianist involved a competition which I felt much too grand ever to consider facing. I couldn't conceive of myself ruthlessly competing against other seventeen-year-olds who quite probably played the piano much better.

INTERVIEWER: Do you have some kind of personal motto that helps you get through your rough moments?

GOULD: During my second tour of Europe I was terribly depressed. I was going to be there for three months, terribly out of touch with all the life that I knew, and everything seemed ridiculous and I wished I were home. Before the first concert, which was in Berlin, I was walking to the rehearsal and suddenly said to myself, "Well, who the hell said it was supposed to be fun anyway?" I must say this pulled me through several weeks. I settled on it as a motto.

INTERVIEWER: Your recording of Bach's *Goldberg Variations* a few years ago suddenly made you a piano celebrity. What did success as a pianist—which you say you had not really sought—mean to you?

GOULD: Well, it meant a great deal to me. But it also launched me into the most difficult year I have ever faced. Up until that time I had not regarded any of the things attendant upon my playing—my eccentricities, if you like—as being of any particular note at all. No one made any fuss about them. Then suddenly a number of well-meaning concert managers and people in the arts wrote to me and said, "My dear young man, you must pull yourself together and stop this nonsense."

INTERVIEWER: What "nonsense"?

GOULD: The fact that I tend to sing a great deal while I'm playing, that I tend to conduct myself with one hand—all that sort of thing. But the point was that all my playing had been done for myself at home, or occasionally in radio studios. Not having been a child prodigy giving concerts, I had never given a thought to the importance, at least to some people, of visual image. When I suddenly was made aware of this in about 1956, I became extremely self-conscious about everything I did. The whole secret of what I had been doing was to concentrate exclusively on realizing a conception of the music, regardless of how it was physically achieved. This new self-consciousness was very difficult, but it was a passing thing.

INTERVIEWER: If you are now less self-conscious, does that mean that you now enjoy playing concerts more?

GOULD: To this day I'm really comfortable only in the studio media—radio and television, or recordings, which I love. I'm quite inured now to playing in public, but I don't really enjoy it. I don't like the one-chance aspect of it.

INTERVIEWER: Some people feel that one of the joys of listening to music arises from the "one-chance" risk of performance—that no one, neither player nor listener, knows quite how it will come out.

GOULD: To me this is heartless and ruthless and senseless. It is exactly what prompts savages like Latin Americans to go to bullfights. When I hear it I want to retire. The spectator in the arena who regards musical performance as some kind of athletic event is happily removed from the risk, but he takes some kind of glee in what goes on there. This is entirely separate from what is really going on: an effort by the performer to form a powerful identification with the music. A performance is not a contest but a love affair. Occasionally something quite lovely will happen at a

concert, of course, and then I'll wish the audience were twenty thousand instead of two thousand. But these moments are very rare. I love recording because if something lovely does happen, there is a sense of permanence, and if it doesn't happen, one has a second chance to achieve an ideal.

INTERVIEWER: Then you have no objection to splicing tapes from several performances into one?

GOULD: I can honestly say that I use splicing very little. I record many whole movements straight through. But I can also say that I have no scruples about splicing. I see nothing wrong in making a performance out of two hundred splices, as long as the desirable result is there. I resent the feeling that it is fraudulent to put together an ideal performance mechanically. If the ideal performance can be achieved by the greatest amount of illusion and fakery, more power to those who do it. I think there is far too much nonsense about the authentic—with all its limitations—being the thing that counts.

INTERVIEWER: Don't you miss the stimulus of an audience in a studio?

GOULD: As I said, my career was spawned in a radio studio. I became used to having the microphone as a friend and a witness to what I do. I've never felt any real stimulus from an audience. The applause of one audience may produce more decibels than another, but coming from a very conservative town such as Toronto, I've learned that noise doesn't necessarily mean true appreciation. I admit that when I was in Israel, where all the audiences are extremely enthusiastic—discerning, too, I think, but nevertheless extremely demonstrative—I had the distinct feeling that another two weeks of this would turn my head completely and that it was about time I got out of there. I would rather be totally indifferent toward the audience. My close friends and relatives, for example, know that I don't like them to attend my concerts. I don't want to have to live up to someone's prior notion of what I'm supposed to be.

INTERVIEWER: You speak of striving

for an ideal performance. Do you think an ideal performance is an objective, recognizable matter?

GOULD: Well, certainly it depends on the aura of the occasion, even the atmosphere of the particular month or year or part of your life it happens in. This changes so greatly. I'll give you one example. A few years ago I made a recording of the Bach D minor concerto, and I was extremely happy with it when I made it. One day, two or three years later, I was in my car and turned on my radio to the middle of the first movement of a recording someone had made of the same concerto. It happens that at that time my phonograph at home was out of adjustment and was turning a wee bit too fast, making everything a half tone too high. I knew it because I have absolute pitch. But it added a pleasant glamour, making everything a little bit tight and Toscanini-like. I had become accustomed to hearing my own recording in E-flat, and here was the piece on the radio in D minor and slower than I had remembered hearing it. I began to wonder whose performance it was. I knew the piece had recently been recorded by pianists X, Y, and Z. I thought this one might be X, because it had all his virtues of solidity; whereas when I had recorded it, I had had a very flippant attitude about music. As I listened I began to think, "Why can't I play with this sort of conviction, this discipline that doesn't need any extras?" I was terribly furious with myself. Then the second movement started, and I thought, "*marvelous* tempo." Then I noticed a couple of grace notes that were extremely offbeat, where the principal note is resolved not on the half beat but on the three-eighths beat. Nobody that I know of does this in Bach except me. And then I recognized that this recording was my own. But the moment I did realize it was mine, I began to see all sorts of things wrong with it.

INTERVIEWER: Do you frequently recognize other pianists by certain characteristic styles, or only by their approach to an individual work?

GOULD: That depends. First of all, I

can almost always tell when a pianist is a woman. Women generally have much less control over the upper arm, so they come down with their forearms like this, hammerlike. And it also shows in their rhythmic thinking of the work. There is generally less spinal momentum in a woman's playing because they tend to be more committed, more directly acting upon the keys, rather than feeling above the instrument. I dare say that 99 per cent of the time I can identify Artur Schnabel, who was my idol when I was a kid and in some ways still is. His characteristic is that he would be almost wholly unconscious of the pianistic resource and would make no attempt to exploit it at all, but, rightly or wrongly, he would use the piano to convey his own peculiar analysis of what he was playing.

INTERVIEWER: When you listen to your recordings, do you recognize your own playing?

GOULD: Yes, by the clarity of the work in architectural terms. First of all, I have never been fond of exploiting the dynamic potentials of the piano. I use almost no pedal at all, and as an old organist I tend to see everything as it relates to the bass line. When the bass line, as in the case of some nineteenth-century music, is not as strong as I would like it, I tend to distort it, deliberately. I delay it, pull it back, use all sorts of tricks to make it strong. As an organist, I think of the cello line, or left-hand line, as being played by the feet. To this day, when I read an orchestral score I tend to move my feet about like this for the bass line—nothing but pedal technique for the organ. Because I started at the organ very young, I still think of music as being played by three hands—the feet acting as the third hand. So I think of music as more contrapuntally divisible than pianists generally do.

INTERVIEWER: Do you learn anything from your own recordings?

GOULD: I sometimes wonder what people did before the invention of the tape recorder. For myself, the only real practicing I do—I do very little—is simply recording things and then listening to them, drawing not only general conclusions but very specific and detailed thoughts about what I am doing and not doing. About eight years ago I did a broadcast of a Beethoven sonata—the Opus 7, No. 4—which has a magnificent slow movement. I had it taped off the air, and next morning I listened to the playback. I couldn't find the metrical shape of the music—I couldn't even beat time to myself. This was strange, because it didn't seem to lack rhythm in my inner mind while I was playing it. I began recording this movement on my own tape recorder several times, and listening back, to see what I could do to correct this. Finally, I found out that in a work of very slow tempo I tended to wait too long before moving toward the next chord. At the point where I should strike the chord, I would be flexing my muscles for it. By that time it was too late. Then, by way of a great revelation, I found I was doing this in many other pieces. It was a serious discovery—and taught me that what you hear internally is not necessarily what is coming out.

INTERVIEWER: In your public playing you have conspicuously avoided the great body of romantic music of the early nineteenth century—Chopin, Schumann, and so forth. What is your quarrel with this music?

GOULD: Basically an architectural one. It isn't tight enough, not organized as scrupulously as I like music—or anything—to be. And it isn't poetic enough. There isn't as strong a metrical pulse as I like music to have. Take, in contrast, Richard Strauss. Here you have a composer using the most varied dramatic palette, but organizing it structurally so that every cadence rhymes with every other cadence. There is a tremendous sense of fulfillment in Strauss. For me, he is one of the great figures of all time. In this aspect of his writing he is a twentieth-century Mozart, in my opinion.

INTERVIEWER: But it is said that you don't like Mozart.

GOULD: It isn't that I don't like Mozart. There are certain aspects of Mozart that attract me greatly. He has a structural tightness around the main pillar that I admire tremendously. The structure of his endings is incomparable. But what I think Mozart lacks—that Haydn had, for instance—is a sense of variation, of relief, while keeping the inner workings active. Mozart doesn't activate all the small details. He throws in more things than are necessary, then doesn't employ everything that is there. But Haydn does. There is, by the way, a concept of me as someone who likes nothing between Bach and Schoenberg except for a few stopovers on the way. This is totally wrong. I am immensely influenced by late romantic music and always have been—Mahler, Strauss, and early Schoenberg. The trouble is that the late nineteenth century is badly represented on the piano. I only wish there were a substantial repertoire of piano music of the late nineteenth-century composers that I really admire. I have the most hair-raising piano transcriptions of Strauss tone poems that you'll ever hear. I play them privately. I've done my own transcription of the overture and last scene of *Capriccio*, Strauss's last opera. It's the most beautiful work this man ever wrote. It's the greatest opera of the twentieth century. I really honestly believe it.

INTERVIEWER: I have heard that you may record the Grieg concerto.

GOULD: We've talked about it. If I do it, it will be out of family pride. He's a relative, a first cousin of my mother's grandfather.

INTERVIEWER: Do you like the piece?

GOULD: It's certainly a piece that—given all my convictions—ought not to appeal to me. I have tried to convince myself that I have a duty to perform in doing it. It is usually played in a fashion that is nine parts traditional and only one part the imagination of the person who happens to be doing it. It is a three-generation hand-me-down and has become incredibly exaggerated from what is really in the score.

INTERVIEWER: Will this open the door to your playing other pieces from the romantic repertoire?

GOULD: I have just done a whole album of Brahms intermezzi, which is the sexiest interpretation of Brahms intermezzi you have ever heard.

INTERVIEWER: How do you mean, "sexiest"?

GOULD: I have captured, I think, an atmosphere of improvisation which I don't believe has ever been represented in Brahms recordings before. There is a quality as though—this isn't an original comment, but something one of my friends said—as though I were really playing for myself, but left the door open. I think a lot of people are going to hate it, but—

INTERVIEWER: But you love it?

GOULD: Yes, I love it. This is one of the things I am most proud of. I am also thinking of making a recording next year of Mendelssohn organ sonatas, which will be a shock to everybody. I adore Mendelssohn. He is a much greater composer than Schumann, for instance, who has an infinitely greater reputation as a serious person. I regard Schumann as one of the weakest figures in major music. Yet one has to be fair and say that there are many people who play Schumann with great conviction and see positive virtues in what I regard as defects. Why they do so is none of my business. Perhaps they see too much discipline in music, while I feel that discipline makes total sense.

INTERVIEWER: Have you listened to much jazz?

GOULD: Yes, but I'm not a jazz buff, really. In my teens I thought I enjoyed Charlie Parker and so on, but it was a very passing fancy. I have never been to a jazz concert in my life.

INTERVIEWER: Do you think jazz has contributed anything important to American music?

GOULD: I think it has contributed a certain native frenzy which is not unbecoming to our contour. I don't mean to be condescending, but I think the propaganda that jazz and classical music will eventually converge is a lot of hogwash.

INTERVIEWER: Do you find any rhythmic excitement in jazz?

GOULD: I think one could get on a high horse and say that no one ever swung more than Bach.

INTERVIEWER: You are sometimes called the dean of the "cool school"—or the intellectual school—of piano playing. How do you feel about this?

GOULD: I think it is wholly inaccurate. It is predicated on the assumption, I think, that all I like to play is (*a*) baroque music and (*b*) twelve-tone music. This is not true, and even if it were true, it would depend on how one played it. The belief came about because I almost totally avoid the use of pedal and dynamic contrasts, both of which are identified with romantic playing. These absences are taken as some sort of coolness or dispassionateness. This is not the case at all. I have cultivated an agile, linear kind of playing and tactile response simply to be as expressive as possible within a very controlled framework of sound. As a matter of fact, a lot of my playing of Beethoven has drawn fire from critics for being too romantic, so they say, and very unconventional in accent.

INTERVIEWER: Since you dissociate yourself from the label of "cool," how do you define "cool" and "romantic?"

GOULD: I never apply these labels to other people, and I don't think they would apply to anyone I admire. But if I *were* to apply them, I would say the romantic interpreter is one who—without necessarily restricting himself to romantic music—tends to be extraordinarily imaginative about music, possibly to the extent that he distorts its architectural framework. The cool player is one who is literally correct about everything but, perhaps through a lack of imagination, ignores the intangible beauties of the music. It would be incredibly dull.

INTERVIEWER: Some critics have complained that when you are playing a concerto and pausing between solo passages, you sit around looking bored.

GOULD: Perhaps many of the complaints about my manner on the stage are justified, but this one is not. I don't think that any pianist or violinist worth his salt, when playing a work in which he is not engaged the whole time, can suddenly during his pauses give up his responsibility and sit idly by. If I am a little bit more obtrusive than some, it is because I am in some kind of intense relationship to what is going on.

INTERVIEWER: What factors contribute to a performer's playing a work differently at different times?

GOULD: There are many factors—one's own mood, the acoustics of the room. In fact, I need only the substitution of an instrument to cause me to play a work quite differently. I try never to be at war with an instrument but to find some way of negotiating a peace with it. In Israel three years ago I had to play a piano that had a nice sound but an extremely difficult action. At that time the one piano in the world that I related everything to, for better or worse, was a sixty-five-year-old Chickering that I have up in the country in Canada. It is quite unlike almost any other in the world, an extremely solicitous piano with a tactile immediacy almost like a harpsichord's. It gives me a sensation of being so close to the strings and so much in control of everything, whereas modern pianos seem to have power steering—they drive you, instead of the other way around. Now when you are touring and playing different instruments every few days, you can reach a pinnacle of confusion. I arrived at this point after four or five concerts in Israel. Should I continue to bend my physical motions to suit this strange instrument with its wretched action? Or should I try to hypnotize myself into believing that I wasn't playing this piano at all? It was a Sunday afternoon, and I rented a car and drove out to some sand dunes. I sat there for almost an hour, mentally reliving moments of having practiced on my Chickering the Beethoven concerto that I was going to play that night.

INTERVIEWER: How so?

GOULD: I rearranged my whole conception to fit the image of my Chickering and nothing else, of what it meant to move one's fingers, and how far one moved them. I went back to the hotel and changed into tails, desperately holding on to this image—that I was to play the Chickering and no other. I walked on stage that night, still believing it, and after about sixteen bars was scared stiff. The keys were barely going down; I was pressing them only about two-thirds of the way to the bottom. The notes were playing all right, but they were coming out tinkly—as though I were really playing that Chickering. After four or five minutes I was leaning in very close to the keys, playing on a smaller dynamic scale than I had played the same work previously. All of the notes fell into clear, rhythmic place, which they had not done in my previous performances on this instrument. I began to enjoy this sort of sound and relaxed. I began to feel at some very great distance from the piano and not at all responsible to it, that I was setting my own terms and simply realizing a muscular expression that suited the music. I went off stage feeling rather pleased with myself but realizing that I didn't know what the hell I was going to do the next night. I couldn't go on like this indefinitely. Well, anyway, a lady came backstage, one of those sentimental old souls who have to verbalize everything. But she said something that struck me so forcibly as an argument that there *is* a communication of total spirit between performer and audience. I have never forgotten it. She said she had heard me play the same work a few nights before, but that this time I seemed in such an elevated frame of mind, as though I were at a greater emotional distance from everything. And this is exactly what it was—exactly.

INTERVIEWER: Do you feel that a performer's responsibility is to play the music purely as he feels it, or as he thinks the composer felt it?

GOULD: There are a few performers in the happy position of feeling that the way they feel the music is the way the composer felt the music. But sometimes I wonder why we fuss so much about fidelity to a tradition of the composer's generation, and not the performer's—for instance, trying to play Beethoven as Beethoven is supposed to have played it. Schnabel attempted this. Much as I admire Schnabel, I think this was a lot of nonsense because he didn't take into consideration the difference in instruments. He followed the pedaling that some scholars say Beethoven intended, but without realizing that these pedalings mean something totally different on a contemporary instrument. There are many times when I am quite sure Mozart would not approve of what I do to his music. The performer has to have faith that he is doing, even blindly, the right thing, that he may be finding interpretive possibilities not wholly realized even by the composer. This is quite possible. There are examples today of contemporary composers—I'd rather not name them—who are the world's worst interpreters of their own music. I am sure this is because inside themselves they hear so much richness in their music that they don't realize they are not projecting it. They don't realize what a performer must do to enliven something.

INTERVIEWER: You speak so seriously of the interpreter's function, and yet earlier you said that you once considered playing the piano a "superficial thing." Has playing become more essential to you in recent years?

GOULD: In an economic sense, yes. But in the sense of needing or desiring to play in public, not at all. What is essential to me is contact with music, but not executing it in public. Some of my friends scoff at this and say that if I retired from playing at my tender years, within six months I would be back at it. I honestly don't believe this is true. I have had periods of six months

or so playing no concerts at all, and I can tell you it was extremely difficult afterward to get wound up again for playing. I think if I did enforce a retirement of three or four years, I would probably never play in public again.

INTERVIEWER: Then what *is* essential to you?

GOULD: I think quite frankly that part of my rejection of concerts is that I want to consider myself a composer. And I admit that so far there has been much more talk than action. In my twenty-nine years I have written only one work of size that I like, my string quartet. I specialize in unfinished works. I don't write to the end of the first page and quit, as many people do. I write to the next to the last page and then quit. I have, for example, a work sitting around that began as a wood-wind quintet, then altered itself and became a clarinet sonata. It has taken three different forms in the past four years. It is 95 per cent completed. Whenever I pick it up, I find some awfully good things in it. But somehow I allow that last page to elude me. So I have written only one work that really pleases me—the quartet. That does not augur an auspicious future in composition. I suppose I should be trying to learn many aspects of the composing craft, especially about orchestral language. Perhaps I should be more prolific. But I am not yet ready to be unhappy about the fact that I have only written one complete work.

INTERVIEWER: If it is really true that you don't highly value the act of piano performance, how is it that you are so good at it?

GOULD: I said that what I valued in a performance was my own satisfaction rather than anyone else's. I do value that sufficiently so that I want to be happy with what I am doing. And I simply have a great enthusiasm for music and its source, which makes me want to take considerable care in relaying it.

Bernard Asbell is a free-lance writer whose report on musical activity in the Midwest, "Mrs. Landon's Harp," appeared in the September, 1959, HORIZON.

ROADS & INROADS

A 1961 advertisement for a newly built American apartment house boasting "closets big enough for a sports car" suddenly brought to mind a vision not merely of supreme affluence but, far more dazzling, the end of our parking problems. It sounded like a new lease on life—a turkey in every pot, a sports car in every utility closet. The advertisement did not say how to get it there, but that is a question for architects, a tribe notorious for their resourcefulness.

Speaking as one of them, I do not doubt that sooner or later the corridors of our apartment houses will become extensions of our highways. With drive-in restaurants and drive-in banks an unqualified success—Frank Lloyd Wright failed by a hair's breadth to give us the perfect museum, a drive-in Guggenheim— we may yet be able to ride in a car all the way up to a penthouse, in imitation of the lord of the manor who rode his horse up the stairway into the ancestral hall.

Cars and roads keep our civilization on the go. Much as a family feels the need of a couple of cars to keep up with the neighbors, a nation's stature is judged by its strangling net of highways. Hence roads are covering country and town, devouring millions of acres, sterilizing the good earth with asphalt and concrete—a self-inflicted blight which may turn out to be one of the great follies of our century.

Some people with rare, albeit pessimistic, vision have long anticipated the inroads of highways on our lives. Almost five centuries ago, Leonardo da Vinci sketched elevated roads traversing a town at roof level. (The most blasphemous of human follies, the Tower of Babel, is supposed to have been equipped with multilane roads spiraling up to the top.) In the 1930's Le Corbusier proposed, as a cure-all for the traffic jams and housing shortage of South American cities, a sort of Chinese Wall, about a dozen stories high and several miles long, with a speedway on top and apartments below. The American Edgar Chambless had hit on a similar solution with his "Roadtown," an endless building designed in 1910.

Moreover, some of these projects are becoming unpleasant reality. An up-to-date version of Roadtown has been built in Tokyo, and the Babelic towers of Biblical times may furnish the prototype for garages from whose spiral ramps it is only one step to the marriage of highways with the rest of architecture.

What the offspring may look like can be deduced from the model shown opposite of a shopping center now being built in Caracas, Venezuela—the most disquieting exhibit in the architectural field. It is called, with Latin flourish, the "Helicoid of the Tarpeian Rock," a strange name when you remember that, in ancient Rome, condemned criminals were hurled from the original Tarpeian Rock. Despite its bulkiness it is only skin deep; it derives monumentality from a cantilevered road that holds the barely visible architecture in its boa-like grip. Alas, Utopia does not sit well on the hill. Construction is making little progress, and rumor has it that the Helicoid may be turned into a city jail. Which at least would put meaning into the classical allusion.

Architect and social critic, Bernard Rudofsky organized the Museum of Modern Art's circulating exhibition, "Roads."

An early antecedent of the Venezuelan shopping center at right may have been the Tower of Babel, depicted in the fanciful 17th-century engraving shown on the facing page. Actual Babylonian ziggurats had ramps leading to a religious shrine at the top.

Below: In 1910 Edgar Chambless envisioned an endless house looping through the countryside. It had trains in the basement, a walkway on the roof, and apartments in between.

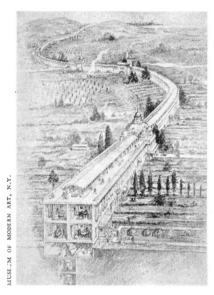

Below: Modern Tokyo has a winding one-way highway and parking roof atop a continuous building which contains shops, offices, and warehouses.

The shopping center planned for Caracas, shown in this model, forms a spiral or helicoid. Enveloping a natural hill, it will have a core of 300 shops around which will wind two and a half miles of alternately ascending and descending one-way roads. Pedestrian walks and parking slots in front of the shops will be protected by the overhang of the circling road.

Total Revolution in the Novel

The latest French model comes stripped of plot, characters, and

even ideas. What's left? Everything that matters, say its creators

By RICHARD GILMAN

"The novel is in the process of reflecting upon itself," wrote Jean-Paul Sartre a few years ago. The observation is the kind one hears only in France, where everything having to do with culture possesses the attributes of sentient life: art suffers, music recoils, poetry commits incest. But even if we wish to avoid the pathetic fallacy, it remains true that novelists, at least, have been reflecting in France and that the results of their meditations have been increasingly visible in the form of books that threaten a revolution in the art of fiction.

French literature, more than any other, has a history of successive repudiations, of a self-conscious shunting aside of established forms and an almost obsessive quest for new ones. From the romantic movement through the naturalists, the symbolists, and the *déracinés,* to the surrealists and the "novelists of engagement," the last hundred and fifty years have witnessed periodic stakings-out of new literary territory, invariably accompanied by furious denunciations of the ground left behind.

But it is doubtful if any previous epoch of French innovation matches the present one in the severity of its ambitions, the self-confidence of its procedures, and the thoroughness with which it supports its imaginative advances with the most passionately argued and systematic body of theory. "This new literature," says Alain Robbe-Grillet, one of its chief architects, ". . . is going to represent—in its fulfillment—a revolution more total than those from which such movements as romanticism and naturalism were born."

Let us take up an example of this new literature, which in France has received a dozen names and finally come to rest a little uneasily under one—the *nouveau roman.* Here is a passage from Robbe-Grillet's novel *The Voyeur* (1955; English-language edition, 1958), a shocking, intricately constructed story of murder and obsession:

It was the last house as he left town. . . . The preliminaries had gone very fast: the brother working for the steamship line, the wrist watches at prices defying all competition, the hallway splitting the house down the middle, the door to the right, the big kitchen, the oval table in the middle of the room, the oilcloth with the many-colored little flowers, the pressure of his fingers on the suitcase clasp, the cover opening back, the black memorandum book, the prospectuses, the rectangular frame on top of the sideboard, the shiny metal support, the photograph, the sloping path, the hollow on the cliff sheltered from the wind, secret, calm, isolated as if by thick walls . . . as if by thick walls . . . the oval table in the middle of the room, the oilcloth with the many-colored little flowers, the pressure of his fingers on the suitcase clasp, the cover opening back as if on a spring, the black memorandum book, the prospectuses, the shiny metal frame, the photograph showing . . . the photograph showing the photograph, the photograph, the photograph, the photograph. . . .

It is clear that we are in the presence of fictional qualities and intentions which are unfamiliar and disconcerting, to say the least. The epithet *chosisme,* or "thingishness," has been applied to Robbe-Grillet's writing, and indeed the catalogue of objects we have just read suggests an obsession with nouns at the expense of other elements of the novelist's usual vocabulary. But the passage also reveals a repetitiveness and a hallucinatory shifting of focus that are equally prominent aspects of Robbe-Grillet's fictional methods.

Nathalie Sarraute is second only to Robbe-Grillet as an exemplar of the new fiction. Here is a paragraph from her *Portrait of a Man Unknown* (1956; English edition, 1958), a kind of detective story in which the quarry is the real existence of "others," the reality behind human surfaces:

Rich ornaments, warm colors, soothing certainties, the fresh sweetness of "life," are not for me. When, occasionally, these "live" persons, or these characters, condescend to come near me too, all I am able to do is to hover about them and try with fanatical eagerness to find the crack, the tiny crevice, the weak point, as delicate as a baby's fontanelle, at which I seem to see something that resembles a barely perceptible pulsation suddenly swell and begin to throb gently. I cling to it and press upon it. And then I feel a strange substance trickling from them in an endless stream, a substance as anonymous as lymph, or blood, an insipid liquid that flows through my hands and spills. . . . And all that remains of the firm, rosy, velvety flesh of these "live" persons is a shapeless gray covering, from which all blood has been drained away.

This seems at first a more conventional piece of writing than the passage from Robbe-Grillet, at least to the degree that its apparent rendering of a psychopathic state is not entirely outside our literary experience. Yet the grotesqueness of the imagery and the extreme hyperbole of the mood indicate that something more is intended than an exercise in medical reportage. A strange new vision of existence is being offered; and we have only to pick up one of Mme Sarraute's novels—*Tropismes, Martereau,* or *The Planetarium*—and read in it at random to discover that the nightmarish yet at the same time ruthlessly derisory quality of the foregoing lines is present in everything she writes, and in fact constitutes her literary identity.

Before heading into the jungles of the *nouveau roman* it may be useful to consider something of its background. Despite their differences, the two authors whose work we have quoted, together with their fellow practitioners, are united by their opposition to the "traditional," or "bourgeois," novel. This is the way with revolutionaries: they always find themselves in closer agreement on what is to be destroyed than on what should be built upon the leveled places. "The positive elements are distinct for each one of us," Robbe-Grillet has written. "And if a certain number of novelists may be looked on as forming a group, this is due much more to their negative elements or to the refusals they make vis-à-vis the traditional novel."

For the *nouveaux romanciers* the traditional novel is the novel of Balzac, which despite its modifications and extensions in the hands of succeeding literary generations, remains the norm and standard of fictional achievement. It is fiction based on a parallelism to life, proceeding the way

experience is supposed to proceed; it is coherent, chronological, dramatic—a "story," in other words. Its chief impulse is to afford knowledge, its chief structural reliance is upon character and plot.

But what has happened in the last hundred years is that much of the sort of knowledge once provided by the novel has been flowing toward us from other sources. The discoveries of the philosophers, the physicists, and the social scientists (especially Freud) have made contemporary man suspicious of fictional attempts to teach him about the world. And this suspicion is reflected in the novel's own effort, as exemplified by Joyce, Proust, Kafka, and Faulkner, to reconstitute itself upon some other basis than that of social, political, or straightforward psychological reality.

But nothing moves in a straight line. In France the immediate predecessor of the *nouveau roman* was not the novel of aloof, self-contained exploration like those of Gide or Proust, or of private myth like those of the surrealists; it was the novel of "engagement," the employment of fiction as a weapon in the social and political struggles of the age, as exemplified by Malraux, Sartre, and Camus. Historically, engagement as a literary motive emerged from a world politicized to an unprecedented degree, in which "fact" impinged drastically on every consciousness and all values were threatened. Yet the novel of engagement was short-lived in France. Malraux turned to a role as self-appointed curator of the world's museums; Sartre gave up fiction for the theater; and even Camus, before his death, showed evidence of a retreat from commitment and from the employment of the novel as an instrument of political salvation.

The new novelists wish to rescue the novel from its suffocation under a weight of accumulated social and political meaning and from its suicidal rivalry with scientific methods of gaining knowledge. They want to destroy fiction's role as mirror of the external world, as well as its function as clinical investigator of the passions and the psyche. And they believe that only when the novel ceases to be a source of illusion—that of possible existences beyond our own—can it hope to revivify itself.

For these reasons the new novelists have announced the death of the fictional "character," with whom the reader has traditionally identified, but who has become lifeless because he is increasingly the incarnation of abstract moral, psychological, or philosophical data derived from an a priori idea of human nature. Their obituary notice extends to plot, which, Mme Sarraute has written, "winds itself around the character like wrappings, giving it, along with an appearance of cohesiveness and life, mummy-like stiffness." The bell tolls, too, for "ideas" in fiction insofar as they are intended to persuade or instruct, and for chronology, which belies the way we actually experience time (because it imposes a linear, cause-and-effect progression upon events, whereas Freud and others have shown that our inner life treats events as coexistent, no matter how far apart they are in time).

What is left? That which is still unknown, Mme Sarraute says. She wishes "to show the existence of contradictory emotions and to reproduce as closely as possible the wealth and complexity of the world of the psyche." The word "reproduce" is of the highest significance here; like all the new novelists she avoids any suggestion of psychological *analysis*.

There are, of course, "characters" in her books—that is to say, men and women who act, speak, and have emotions. But they are scarcely personages or personalities; they have not been endowed with orthodox novelistic existence, complete with a history, a destiny, and a set of recognizable features. Instead they inhabit a work in somewhat the same way as shapes and masses inhabit an abstract painting (the comparison is frequently stressed in the new literature's theoretical writings), as essences rather than particularized beings or objects: instead of a red flower in an abstract paint-

Alain Robbe-Grillet

ing we have *redness*; instead of a jealous man in one of these new novels we have *jealousy*. These qualities are emanations from the psychic world of the novelist, and they come into contact with one another, collide, interpenetrate, or ricochet, the way the rich and ambivalent life of the mind organizes its own movements.

There is also little more than a semblance of conventional plot in Mme Sarraute's books. Almost nothing *happens*: in *Portrait of a Man Unknown* a youth probes the relationship between an old man and his daughter; in *Martereau* (1953; English edition, 1959) a family friendship is furtively explored; in *The Planetarium* (1959; 1960) an aspiring writer tries to force his aunt to give him her large apartment. Yet all three novels—difficult to read in the absence of conventional landmarks, irritating, inconclusive, with an atmosphere like that of subterranean chambers—do possess an extraordinary fascination and at their best impart a sense of

having entered uncharted territory.

The fascination derives from the revelations that flow from Mme Sarraute's scrutiny of precisely those aspects of our relations to others and our sense of self that we ordinarily consider beneath notice, "those lowly nuances where now and then lies the truth." Sartre called her a "soul-detective," but she is less interested in what we think of as the soul than in that "infra-psychological" reality which is present in our smallest gestures and responses, and which constitutes a mocking voice in the face of our grandiose opinions, attitudes, and conscious values.

To force this "new psychological matter" into the light, Mme Sarraute works at cracking the shell that covers our day-to-day activities, the carapace of our conventional behavior. Her principal tool is a vocabulary whose violence is in almost direct proportion to the ostensible insignificance of what is being dealt with. The most innocuous-seeming encounters are described in images drawn from the embattled, voracious life of insects and animals, from the lexicon of disease, of military action, or of physical disaster.

The colorless old man and his daughter in *Portrait of a Man Unknown* are engaged in the "blind, relentless struggle of two giant insects, two enormous dung beetles." At the approach of an acquaintance Martereau feels "something limp, prehensile, floating, borne toward him on the current, flabby tentacles ready to reach out toward him, all their cups opening avidly to cling to him, to suck. . . ." In *The Planetarium* a socially intimidated youth feels "shattered, done for. Now he's like a little boat with a thin, fragile bottom that a big ship has run into, ripped open, he's bursting on all sides, he's about to sink. . . ."

Along with this feral, catastrophic imagery, whose effect is to startle us into an awareness of a life seething beneath the surface, Mme Sarraute employs another kind—bland, domestic, tame, yet poisonous with irony. Its purpose is to hold up to ridicule the pretense we make of having mastered our fates and to eject us from our illusions of well-being and happiness. The young couple of *The Planetarium* has bought a new sofa:

Only marriage permits such moments as these, of fusion, of happiness, during which, leaning on him, she had gazed at the old silk with its ash-rose, its delicate gray tones, the large nobly spreading seat, the broad back, the free, firm curve of the elbow-rests . . . a caress, a consolation emanated from its calm ample lines . . . this was beauty, harmony itself, captured, subjugated, familiar, become part and parcel of their life, a joy constantly within their reach.

Mme Sarraute's intention is double: to compel the truth behind appearances to reveal itself, and to overthrow the reign in literature of the "significant" idea, the presanctified value, and the categorized emotion. She is saying that most of what we think and feel is inauthentic, and a literature that is not continually purging itself of the known tends to confirm us in our borrowed gestures instead of freeing us.

Alain Robbe-Grillet is also concerned with the authentic and its opposite. But where Mme Sarraute deals with human relations, in however transmogrified a way, his novels seem to present us with an image of the naked, isolated individual in a dehumanized universe. Robbe-Grillet has been hailed as perhaps the most important innovator in the novel's history, and has also been damned with a fury not exceeded by that

Nathalie Sarraute

once directed against James Joyce. For in his hands the novel loses almost all resemblance to anything we are accustomed to, while opening up, for those patient enough to persevere in the face of its undeniable difficulties, a perspective on something unprecedentedly bold and revealing.

What we have earlier called Robbe-Grillet's "thingishness" is not a preoccupation with objects in the usual sense but with their presence after they have been stripped of the encrustations, the "fringe of culture," which we are continually adding to them, thereby destroying their real strangeness and making them inauthentic. Things exist before our interpretations of them, Robbe-Grillet argues, and they continue to exist independently of the associations we make with them.

In the novel of the future, things will simply *be there,* and man will come to know them, and through them his own situation, by direct confrontation and without recourse to any explanatory frame of reference. The novelist has heretofore functioned, Robbe-Grillet says, as a species of speleologist, or cavern explorer, burrowing into nature in search of its "romantic heart"; but the new novelist will be content to roam the surface, reporting only what he sees and resisting all impulses to harness the world to his own emotions through metaphor and the protective adjectives by which we tame the unknown.

A further cause of the distortion of our experience, Robbe-Grillet asserts, is time, which forces events into a pattern of causality and imposes an unjustifiable logic upon them. To

escape linear time—chronology—he constructs what we might call *psychological* time, in which events happen simultaneously, without progression and therefore without change. This Einsteinian mixture of time and space dominates all of Robbe-Grillet's work.

His novels, it may be imagined, make no concession to the reader. The latter finds himself straining constantly after that connection with the world through metaphor and that step-by-step progress through time to which the ordinary novel has accustomed him. He is in a landscape without signposts, where the air is icy, the sky a flinty blue, and where what he sees is presented to him without depths and without justifications or criticisms.

In both *The Voyeur* and *Jealousy,* Robbe-Grillet's major novels, there is a central figure and an "action" to which he is related: an itinerant salesman in *The Voyeur* commits, or thinks he has committed (we are never sure which), a rape-murder; a suspicious husband in *Jealousy* (1957; 1959) watches the progress of what may or may not be an affair between his wife and a neighbor. The indefiniteness of both actions is a function of Robbe-Grillet's shift of attention from events as they take place in actuality to their existence in the mind, in memory, where experience is frozen and preserved from time.

We are kept firmly within this psychological time by the manner in which events are described without obedience to the order in which they normally would have occurred, and by the frequent repetitions in which the same action is subjected to different emphases and made to reveal new perspectives. Together with this is the fact that the objects and gestures in the novel are forced to remain static, evoking nothing but their outlines and mysterious presence. Consider these paragraphs from *The Voyeur:*

Then the man slowly approaches, stands behind her, stares at her for a moment, stretches out his hand, and slowly caresses the nape of her neck with his fingertips. The huge hand, the blond head, the oil lamp, the edge of the first plate (on the right), and the left upright of the window are all aligned in the same oblique plane.

The lamp is made of brass and clear glass. From its square base rises a cylindrical, fluted stem supporting the oil reservoir —a half-globe with its convexity underneath. This reservoir is half-full of a brownish liquid. . . . On its upper part is a flange of stamped metal an inch and a half high, into which is screwed the glass, a perpendicular tube widening slightly at the base. It is this perforated flange . . . which can be seen most clearly of all the articles in the room. It consists of two superimposed series of equal tangent circles—rings, more exactly, since their centers are hollow—each ring of the upper series being exactly above a ring of the lower row to which it is joined for a fraction of an inch.

The first paragraph concerns the beginning of a terrifying crime, one that the reader has already been made aware of in other shapes. The effect of the abrupt transition to the meticulous, absolutely emotionless description of the lamp

DRAWINGS BY NICHOLAS SOLOVIOFF

Michel Butor

is that our feelings, previously aroused to a high pitch, are not allowed to *drain off* into the setting and that we are forced to rebound, as it were, from the smooth walls of the object depicted, back to the locus of psychic reality, the crime as it echoes in the mind of the onlooker-protagonist.

In both novels the reader finds his consciousness merging with that of the protagonist. In *The Voyeur* the union is incomplete, since the salesman, although denuded of personality, is still visibly on stage and participates in outward events. But in *Jealousy* everything occurs entirely within the protagonist's consciousness; he never appears or refers to himself, so that the "story" of the novel is nothing more nor less than the *mental content*, during an indefinite period of great strain, of this man who remains unknown to us in every other way.

This mental content, this condition of morbid jealousy, becomes literally our own, since there is nothing separating the fictional character from ourselves. The same handful of images—a centipede crushed against a wall, a wife brushing her hair, the neighbor holding his cocktail glass—recur again and again, seen from different vantage points, subjected to new intensities, transposed, arranged in new sequences, so that they come to exist simultaneously. At the same time the images are related to each other in a chain that links up separate sensory realms:

The car immediately bursts into flames. The whole brush is *illuminated* by the crackling, spreading fire. It is the *sound* the centipede makes, motionless again on the wall . . . listening to it more carefully, this sound is more like a breath than a crackling: the brush is now moving down the loosened hair. [Italics added.]

The fictional techniques employed in *Jealousy* may be said to deliberately narrow the range of the novel in order to apply a purer and more intense vision to the area that remains. Within this chosen region Robbe-Grillet is able to achieve the most powerful effects of immediacy, with the result that he seems to have opened up some new dimension of experience that exists beneath the processes of reflection,

rationalization, and mythologizing by which we habitually deform even our most central activities.

Robbe-Grillet's critics, it has to be said, reject all this, and with the utmost virulence. There is a widespread charge that he "competes with the land-registry," that is, that he composes mere lists, multiplying details to no significant purpose. More serious is the argument that he "dehumanizes" the novel, turning it into a soulless document. To this Robbe-Grillet has replied, "How can they . . . accuse a novel of turning against or away from man when it follows from page to page each one of his steps, describing only what he does, what he sees or what he imagines?"

What seems clear is that Robbe-Grillet has really turned away from psychological analysis, the most fashionable element of contemporary fiction, in order to create psychology afresh. And his abandonment of the entire corpus of formal values, aspirations, soul-searchings, and neural malaise in which fictional man has been located, is no doubt what so irritates his detractors. For the novel in his hands is no longer, as Roland Barthes remarks, "a chthonian revelation, the book of hell, but of the earth," and no longer the world seen from the viewpoint of "a confessor, a doctor, or God himself," but of a man "with no other power than that of his own eyes."

Although Robbe-Grillet and Nathalie Sarraute dominate critical discussion of the *nouveau roman*, there are other French novelists who share their rejection of fictional orthodoxies and their restless search for new techniques. Samuel Beckett is certainly the best known of them, but Michel Butor and Marguerite Duras, to name only the most interesting, constitute a second echelon of the movement.

Michel Butor has described the novel as a "new kind of epic and didactic poetry," every new subject demanding a discovery in technique. The outward subject of his *La Modification* (which has sold more than 100,000 copies, making it by far the biggest popular success of the new literature; it has been published here in 1959 under the title *A Change of Heart*) is the overnight rail journey which a Parisian businessman is taking to Rome in order to tell his Italian mistress that he has decided to leave his wife for her. Its true subject, however, is the manner in which three levels of human awareness are related: that of the external world; that of our actual history, available in memory; and that of our "mythological" history, our deepest responses and motivations, which lie buried within our unconscious.

Butor's chief innovations are his use of the second person to address his protagonist—"*You* enter the compartment . . . you stretch your legs . . ."—an effective way of implicating the reader in the action; and the interweaving, without regard to chronology or logic, of descriptions of the actual trip, memories of past journeys to Rome, anticipations of the future, and finally, dreamlike passages in which a figure resembling the Great Huntsman of French folklore, an irruption from the depths of the psyche, conducts the traveler on still another journey, a visionary one that leads to the truth.

The "modification" that takes place concerns the rising to the surface of this repressed mythological truth. In the end "you" have abandoned your rigorously achieved plan, for you have discovered that it is not your mistress you really desire but her presence in Rome, and even more than that, Rome itself, which—in its incarnation of art, youth, and beauty—you have needed as a counterforce to Paris, where you are located in family, age, and obligation. To take her back there with you would be to destroy the relationship you have set up between these two geographical foci, which are at the same time contrasting mythologies. All you can do now is "try to bring to life, in the form of literature, this crucial episode in your experience, the movement that went on in your mind while your body was being transferred from one station to another. . . ." That is to say, only literature can correct the distortion of our experience caused by our continual movement through time and space, but it can do this solely by going beyond memory or the immediately actual.

Marguerite Duras is a more conventional novelist than any of the three we have discussed, but within her still recognizable settings and surviving chronologies she carries on experiments which are also attempts to uncover new uses for the novel and new matter for its composition.

Marguerite Duras

She is best known here for her screenplay for the notable film *Hiroshima, Mon Amour,* itself an outstanding product of the new aesthetic in France. In her hands the novel is purified, cleansed, and reduced to its barest essentials. In *The Square* (1955; 1959), where her intentions are perhaps clearest, the action unfolds in a single period of perhaps a few hours and is almost entirely contained within the conversation of two strangers, a young nursemaid and a traveling salesman, who meet on a bench in a public square. We are told nothing about their physical appearances, nor are we given access to their thoughts or emotions except as they are revealed in their speech. Their conversation thus becomes a timeless, fragile forging of contact between two anonymous souls who move from the most remote and accidental of relationships to the birth of sympathy, trust, and an intuition of the potentiality each possesses for love.

They are lonely, hermetic, and passive. Yet each bears a seed of longing for mutuality and involvement, and this is what they encourage in one another. "I'm twenty," the girl says. "Nothing has happened to me yet. I sleep well. But one day I must wake up and forever. It must happen." And the man: "If people feel the need for the sun it is because they know how sad the dark can be. No one can live always in the dark."

As their astonishing conversation ends they have exposed themselves to each other and are poised on the edge of a union based on absolute honesty, refusal of pretense, and the most delicate recognition of man's struggle to accept life and to create his own reality against the pull of oblivion. And these, it may be added, are the qualities and aims of Marguerite Duras's prose.

For all these novels and for those novels of the future that may present themselves in even more disconcerting and refractory shapes, Alain Robbe-Grillet has issued a word of warning and guidance to the reader. "A new form," he writes, "always seems to be more or less an absence of any form at all, since it is unconsciously judged by reference to consecrated forms." To be prepared to deconsecrate his literary idols, to allow the new and unheard-of to mount the stripped pedestals or at least make its presence known alongside the dying gods, is what is being asked of the reader in France, as it has so many times in the past.

And the writer, too, is being challenged. Butor has written that "the novelist who turns his back on this work [of formal innovation], upsetting no set habits, demanding no special effort of his reader, not driving the latter to scrutinize himself and the positions he has long since made his own, is of course going to succeed more easily, but he makes himself the accomplice of our profound discomfort and of the deep night in which we flounder. . . . His work, in the last analysis, is a poison."

Nowhere has the twofold, perhaps impossible, ambition of the new literature been more aggressively stated: to be both nutriment and antidote, to needle and to cure, matching the pace of our advancing confusion and despair with continual discoveries of new means of illuminating our condition and of setting free those human possibilities that never cease clamoring for an opening into the light.

Richard Gilman is the drama critic of Commonweal. *His study of the late Albert Camus, "The Writer as the Conscience of France," appeared in* HORIZON *for November, 1959.*

On Stage: SALOME JENS

A simple haystack of a girl from a Wisconsin dairy farm, with the unlikely name of Salome Jens, is quietly collapsing all the established molds and matrices of Broadway and Hollywood. At twenty-five she is a high-density performer with all of the perquisites but few of the prerequisites of stardom. She wears no make-up, her jaw is squarely set, her eyes bunch too close together, her nose sprawls wide across a peasant face, and she is five feet nine inches tall—a veritable veldt of plainness who cried when she first saw herself on a movie screen "because I looked so ugly."

But Miss Jens was clearly wrestling with what e. e. cummings would call a nonproblem. If at first glance she evokes the specter of a poke-bonneted pioneer woman carved out of Grant Wood Gothic, when she moves and speaks, what was cumbersome and cloddish is suddenly warm, weightless, and confectionary. The eyes lose their bland togetherness and become nervous, glittery blue flames; the whole face floats to sensitive life; the rangy, rawboned form takes on a proud, willowy dazzle; and the voice is purest gold.

It was this miracle of transformation that Miss Jens performed three years ago for her toughest, smallest, and most apprehensive audience, composed of Lee Strasberg, Elia Kazan, and Cheryl Crawford; and in a single five-minute reading landed grandly in the Actors' Studio for life. "I did this big lunky girl who thought she was ugly in *Moon for the Misbegotten*," says Salome, "and the Studio helped with most of the work I've gotten since," e.g., *The Disenchanted*, *A Far Country*, and the movie *Angel Baby*, which led to a five-picture contract in Hollywood. Notwithstanding the indifferent reception of the picture, a sort of road-company *Elmer Gantry*, Salome herself won critical hosannas as the prurient evangelist. But her really salient memory of moviedom turns on the night she read for that part.

"I was doing *The Balcony* in New York [in which her role as the seductive prostitute won her the Clarence Derwent award for 1960], and this director came in afterwards, looked at me hard and said, 'A star is born.' I said I'd heard that before. He asked me to go to a hotel to read for *Angel Baby* for the producer, so I made my sister [actress Arnette Jens, twenty-four, who succeeded Salome in *Balcony*] go with me. It was one o'clock in the morning and they handed me the scene that takes place in the empty revival tent. It reminded me of all the lovely things in my childhood. Emotionally I just went ker-*plook*. They were crying and I was crying and it was lovely."

Although born in Milwaukee and reared on a farm near Hartland, home for Salome is now Waukeska County, where her Polish mother and German father, Salomea Szujewski and Arnold John Jens, operate a resort known as The Jolly Fisherman on an inland lake. As a girl, Salome was variously a movie cashier, Miss Avalon Theater, Miss Bay View Frolic, Miss Wisconsin Flash Bulb, and, with Arnette, one of the dancing Apple Sisters, Seedy and Cora, in state-fair bandstand shows. "When I got all those titles, I began to sympathize with the prize-winning hogs!" From the University of Wisconsin Salome went to Northwestern and put her phenomenal memory to the test on *Uncle Vanya, Six Characters in Search of an Author, Misalliance*, and *The Caucasian Chalk Circle*. In 1956 she went to New York, landed a secretarial post with an advertising firm, and at night studied acting with Herbert Berghof and dance with Martha Graham. "Suddenly everything was fun."

But, Salome recalls, "People always said, 'she's too tall and too funny-looking and we can't cast that girl.' I was always the brassy blonde sexpot doing kookie bits with a high voice and an empty head." *A Far Country* provided her an unspectacular part, but "I had to prove to the people in the theater I could do something else, something controlled and quiet. Sometimes, it's better if you *don't* make a sensation."

Miss Jens's first sensation was in Ionesco's short *The Bald Soprano,* in which, according to Brooks Atkinson, she was "alive in a sea of platitudes" and as "incandescent as a 200-watt bulb." What was there about her background or behind those luminous eyes that helped shape this uncommon talent? "I don't know," says Salome, "and my Mama and Papa don't know either."

At the first screening of *Angel Baby* Allied Artists invited Mama and Papa Jens to New York and encouraged them to bring their relatives. "Well," recalls Salome, "Mama brought over one hundred people and filled the theater. Not even the censors could get in." And recently Mama got the Milwaukee Theater "all sold out" for the local opening of *A Short Happy Life,* A. E. Hotchner's adaptation of several Hemingway stories, with Miss Jens in the part of the heroine. Finally, last December, Salome won her first New York leading role, in Robert Ardrey's *Shadow of Heroes,* a play based on the 1956 Hungarian uprising.

She retains an almost mystical relationship to her profession. "I do think of the theater as a spiritual thing, and I feel an obligation to it. The truest way to explain it is I try to find the moment-to-moment reality of the different situations. This is somehow my whole technique. There is no such thing as Method. Every actor has his own method."

A pause. An appealing tilt of the head. "Once I wanted to be the first woman president of the United States, but now I am happy acting and I think maybe I'll make it."

C. ROBERT JENNINGS

Photograph by BOB WILLOUGHBY

On Stage: WARREN BEATTY

Penrod Schofield is a long time dead; and it would appear that even Harold Teen, though he persisted, did not really survive World War I. As of around 1921 all youth became troubled youth. When our middle-aged dramatists look back on the corn and wheat fields of their childhood, only discouraging words and cloudy skies do they see. It is, in the main, this business of sex that causes all the alarms; it is astonishing to discover how widespread was the canker in our own Midwest. Our playwrights have presented us with two dominant types: one whose masculinity is in doubt; and the other, who has so much of it—"There's something I'd like to talk to you about, Doc"—that it becomes a burden so unbearable that neither Sweet Caporals nor a game of pool can soothe the tormented soul.

Angst-ridden young men have become a commonplace on Broadway; and since last year's theater neuroses are this year's fashion in Hollywood, actors capable of projecting such anxieties find themselves in a sellers' market in films.

Warren Beatty was, therefore, inevitable; it can almost be said that he is a star due to circumstances beyond his control. His rise is as much a matter of genes as of talent or temperament. Beatty *is* the troubled American Boy. He is, like the Arrow-collar man's profile, not an average but an aspiration, a type exaggerated into an individual: he is taller, handsomer, slimmer than any average, and probably brighter.

Born in Richmond, Virginia, he moved soon after to Arlington, that international enclave where no regional accent is allowed to live (he can therefore create his own and change it on demand). To date, he has played two Midwestern boys and one Italian gigolo. His first Midwestern boy was seen on Broadway, briefly, in William Inge's *A Loss of Roses*. The second is currently on view in the film *Splendor in the Grass*, written by Inge and directed by Elia Kazan. And his gigolo may be seen in the film version of Tennessee Williams's *The Roman Spring of Mrs. Stone*, directed by José Quintero.

To play in *A Loss of Roses*—he was just twenty-one then —Beatty not only gave up a contract with MGM but returned to them all the money they had paid him while he waited in Hollywood for the call. He also turned down leading roles in *Parrish* and other films of like quality. Such discrimination as he has shown has rewarded Mr. Beatty handsomely. His next film will be *All Fall Down*, screenplay again by Inge, directed by John Frankenheimer. He has also been offered starring roles in the following expensive properties: Hersey's *The War Lover*; Lampedusa's *The Leopard*; and Moss Hart's *Act One*.

It was Joshua Logan who, during an audition for a now abandoned project, was first struck by Beatty's potential and spoke of him to his friends Inge and Kazan. At that time Beatty had behind him only some television and summer stock appearances and six months of training with Stella Adler. Although Beatty's grandmother had been an elocution teacher and his mother had directed community plays, he does not come from a professional family; but two generations of theater amateurs have reached a sudden flowering: Beatty's older sister is the Hollywood star Shirley MacLaine, who uses their mother's maiden name. In school Beatty was the star not of the drama club but of the football field. On graduation from Washington and Lee High School, he was offered athletic scholarships by ten colleges, but he went off instead to Northwestern University's department of speech.

Beatty returned East after one year at Northwestern, and while studying with Stella Adler supported himself by working on construction jobs until he began to get roles in television. Those were what the new chairman of the Federal Communications Commission now thinks of as the Great Old Days of television, when Kraft Theater and Studio One enriched the government-licensed air; it was a period when, we are asked to believe, television flowered. It was in these heady, creative, maturing days that Beatty first came to the attention of viewers in such memorable, mature, and creative vehicles as *The Curly-Headed Kid* and *The Night America Trembled*. (Surely we all remember *The Curly-Headed Kid* and *The Night America Trembled*?) Beatty apparently was not aware that he was part of a cultural efflorescence; he remembers it only as very hard work.

On his brief Broadway appearance in *A Loss of Roses* the critics cancelled each other out: Mr. Kerr found him "mercurial" and Mr. Atkinson thought him "earnest." Those who have seen *Splendor* find that, as in most Kazan films, the actors have a way of being overwhelmed by the director. The characters in this one live at such a high emotional level that it is a wonder any of them survive to middle age. Beatty, as coached by Kazan, moves with agility through the emotional scrimmage.

Among Beatty's more onerous duties these days is posing for photographs. Entering a photographer's studio recently, he saw under the lights a setup for a whiskey advertisement: a bottle of bourbon and a football ("After the Victory Game . . ."). He passed the ball back and forth with the photographer for a few minutes; then he stopped and looked at it, holding the ball in both hands. "Six years!" he said. "I wasted six years!" He sat on a high stool then, submitting himself to the lights. He held on to the football, looking down at it with wonder, as if it were some exotic token of a past almost beyond recall. WARREN MILLER

Photograph by SAM SHAW

THEATER

The Persistence of Ibsenism

Are we to have an Ibsen revival? In the theater one does not ask such questions —it is like inquiring which way the cat will jump—and I shall venture no more than to say that the idea is plausible and desirable. There are a few signs: David Ross, whose Fourth Street Theater in New York first won acclaim as a Chekhov house, last season presented *Hedda Gabler* in a production that was well praised and well patronized; and he followed it last September with a fine presentation of *Ghosts*. During August, CBS televised scenes from *Brand* on a Sunday morning religious show, and in Provincetown over the Labor Day weekend I watched a young company grapple with the mystic desperations of *When We Dead Awaken*.

David Ross's second Ibsen presentation is much surer than his first. There were good scenes in the *Hedda Gabler*, but the play was made somewhat shallow by a disposition to see Hedda as an ambitious bitch, rather than as the manifestation of perverse romanticism posing as a higher sensibility, about which Ibsen was concerned. The production of *Ghosts,* with Leueen MacGrath (Mrs. Alving), Staats Cotsworth (Manders), and Joseph Marino (Oswald), is staged with taut nerves, painful clarity, and a fine particularity of character. The point that a wife should not be obliged to

cleave to a man who pursues the parlor-maid is no longer controversial, and Miss MacGrath acts to make the play pivot on Mrs. Alving's sense of duty. She understands herself very clearly and very much too late. Ross will surely continue with the cycle, for the reception of the first two plays has been good; and New York will thus be shown, in a converted cold-water flat on the lower East Side, something of the range of the greatest theater mind of the nineteenth century.

But the evidence of a revival is not conclusive, for we have always given sporadic attention to Ibsen. In the past ten years New York has seen twelve productions of seven Ibsen plays, better than one a season. The effort, though, has been scattered, the achievement uneven, the attention minimal: we seem to put on Ibsen when we have nothing more pressing to do. Respect for Ibsen is such that his name is never omitted from the shortest list of theater immortals, but this honor comes close to being one of those hollow forms that so roused Ibsen's own savagery as a playwright. He may be part of our tradition, but he is scarcely part of our life.

I do not suppose, however, that the American theater will be so quixotic as to stage an Ibsen renaissance for the sake of the public's intellectual honesty. On the contrary, and practically speaking,

I think the time is ripe. In particular, it is ripe for Ibsen to stand clear of the protecting cloak Bernard Shaw threw around him. No artist under the attack of ignorance ever enjoyed a more brilliant defense, but Shaw's eloquence now stands between Ibsen and the contemporary audience. Younger than Ibsen, Shaw was nevertheless more specifically a man of the last century: if you will, he was a narrower man. Further, he was disposed to admire people for their ability to agree with him, and he saw in Ibsen the virtues he knew himself to possess—principally social reason and hot indignation.

In those days—1891 and after—Ibsen was being vilified (in the immoderate terms that only the moderate Victorians could employ without embarrassment) for his immorality, and Shaw proved conclusively and repeatedly in *The Quintessence of Ibsenism* that his subject was the most moral of preceptors. Today the suggestion that there is anything wicked in Ibsen can only make us smile. Indeed, it is hard to find in his work anything we would call unconventional. Even more damaging, perhaps, to our interest in the plays was Shaw's relish for his elder's iconoclasm. It is certainly true that Ibsen was a formidable dynamiter who seriously weakened, if he did not finally shatter, a number of revealed truths. But it is fatal today to celebrate him for having challenged the sanctity of marriage, the omniscience of the church, the efficacy of idealism, the probity of constituted authority, the wisdom of the "compact majority." These issues brought out the intellectual militia in the nineties, but Ibsen fairly disposed of them and Shaw mopped up the pockets of resistance. And insofar as they won their battles, that aspect of their work became dated propaganda.

Shaw has become more dated than Ibsen (he now survives principally through his wit) because he was more exclusively a propagandist. His disservice to his hero was that he did not see, or did not sufficiently value, the further depths of the man. The rational, free-thinking socialism, the utopia of the syllogism, that so preoccupied Shaw was not the only wind of promise flowing across Europe in the latter half of the nineteenth century. Ibsen was born in 1828, Freud in 1856. During the span of the playwright's career, from 1848 to 1900, the psyche was coming ever more sharply under the microscope, and though there is not, so far as I know, a single psychoanalytic reference in the plays, they are all of them—and increasingly as the work accumulates—concerned with the functions and maladies of the ego. In that respect, Ibsen is as much our contemporary as Shaw's.

Today, of course, the theater steams with psychology: whole scenes are devoted to group analysis, and one can almost detect which of the Freudian sects a playwright's analyst adheres to by listening to the prattle of the characters.

I doubt that this tendency is good for the stage, or for any other form of narrative in which it takes strong hold. It acts to reduce people to case histories and turns drama into a clinical monograph. We no longer concern ourselves with good and evil, but with putting the right tag on a neurosis. This not only vulgarizes Freud, but pitifully diminishes the human experience.

No one in Ibsen sports a neurosis. His characters struggle against Fortune as though they were men and women of free will and sound mind, assumptions that must be made if we are to struggle at all. But, strictly speaking, Ibsen did not portray a single victim: one and all, his people bring their own wrath down upon themselves. Sometimes they know it, as does Mrs. Alving in *Ghosts* by the time Oswald asks her for the sun; some-

As They Saw the Theater's Norseman

Four irreverent sketches portray Ibsen in the 1890's, when he was considered both the aging bad boy and the father-figure of European theater. Left: "Mr. Punch's Pocket Ibsen" was drawn by Bernard Partridge; the rear view (below) appeared in The Critic; *right: Max Beerbohm acidly depicted "Ibsen receiving Mr. William Archer in audience"—note wallpaper pattern; below right: Schmitt caricatured the "Jubilee banquet to Dr. Ibsen," with worthies attending to honor his seventieth birthday.*

times, as in *The Master Builder*, the revelation is itself fatal; and sometimes, as in *An Enemy of the People*, the curtain falls with the hero plunging still deeper into the delusions of his private night.

An Enemy of the People is an apt example of the persistence of Ibsenism. It scorches alike the wickedness of entrenched commercial power and the prudence of popular opposition. Shaw hailed it in those terms, but who today would cross the street to see a play teaching that bureaucrats will behave monstrously to save their shirts and that their opposition can be routed by the cry of higher taxes?

Consider, however, the personal behavior of the protagonist. Why should Dr. Stockmann, that high-minded and public-spirited man, fall into such a merry humor when he discovers that the medicinal waters on which his town depends for its prosperity are dangerously polluted? Why does he hasten to a newspaper with the sad facts; why does he rub his hands and talk excitedly of smiting, crushing, and beating to the ground? The fact is he hates his older brother and is overjoyed to surprise him with his hand in the cookie jar. Dr. Stockmann was not looking to improve matters; he was looking to provoke a fight, and his tragedy was that he no longer had a mother to run to. *An Enemy of the People* fascinates today, long after its social message has been absorbed, because its hero is not only the play's voice of conscience but its principal villain. It answers a question that we ask ourselves with almost every morning's newspaper: Why are reformers so often more unappetizing than the rascals they pursue?

Shaw commends *Rosmersholm* to us as a demonstration of love's evolution from a lower (animal) to a higher (rational) form, but since the play ends with a suicide pact in the mill race, I suspect that a modern director could define more precisely the relationship between Rebecca West and John Rosmer. Similarly, Shaw praises *A Doll's House* for contributing to the emancipation of wives from domestic tyranny. It certainly does that, but it also comes to the aid of husbands whose wives insist on pretending that the marriage bed is a play pen. Nora not only permits such endearments as "twittering lark" and "bustling squirrel," she gives the impression of encouraging them as part of the Helmers' mating rites. If so, the ensuing intimacies must take a form that does Torvald no good at all. This, however, is not the sort of speculation that would have occurred to Shaw.

I could, I think, show similarly that the psychological aberrations of relatively normal men and women lie at the base of every Ibsen play, and I feel sure that the way to deliver them alive to the stage today is to ask, not what social institution is here under attack, but what is eating the characters. A fault, perhaps, in Ibsen's psychological insights is that he sometimes failed to appreciate how stubborn a neurosis can really be—he lacked, after all, the clinical reports of those long years on the couch. Thus, in *The Pillars of Society*, it is more surprising than convincing that Karsten Bernick, after a lifetime of rationalization so extreme that he can evade the guilt of sending a ship to almost certain death, should in the last scene make an open and healing confession of his lies.

But that, relatively, was an early play. Contrast it with *Little Eyolf*, a much later work, which offers perhaps the most poignant happy ending in modern drama. Alfred and Rita Allmers seek reconciliation and tranquility in a philanthropy dedicated to the memory of their dead son, not realizing that the dagger that lies between them is not guilt for the little boy's lameness (he was injured when they left him unattended to embrace each other) but Alfred's unacknowledged realization that his wife's physical vitality is more significant than his creative energy. Ibsen's whole work is permeated with the torments occasioned by the illusions and frustrations of the creative process.

And Ibsen's whole work is what should now concern us—not a play this season to fill out a repertory and another next season because an actress would like to try her hand at playing Rebecca West in *Rosmersholm*. We should not pick about among his works to find something that suits us, but should trust him to be the genius we so glibly proclaim him and give him the freedom of our stage.

I would not be taken too literally: even Shakespeare does not survive intact. Ibsen wrote ten plays before *Brand* brought him fame in 1866, and I doubt that those early works, based for the most part on sagas and Norse history, could be reanimated. *Brand* is possibly too single-minded and too daemonic for our domestic stage (although it would make a compelling opera); and *Emperor and Galilean*, that Gargantuan double drama which sprawls across the Roman Empire and spends whole armies in the search for a Caesar's soul, might overtax our physical resources as well as our philosophic energies. It could be made into the greatest of all Biblical screen extravaganzas, but at what cost to its core of meaning I will not attempt to estimate.

Beginning, however, with *Peer Gynt* (that terrible portrait of the charming, talented, half-baked man) and skipping the sanguinary pilgrimage of the Emperor Julian, there are fourteen plays for an Ibsen theater. They range from the farce of *The League of Youth* to the tragic dirge of *John Gabriel Borkman;* they are in prose and poetry. (They are not, however, all adequately translated: Ibsen has not yet escaped entirely from the timidly accurate, much annotated trots of William Archer.) Ibsen's job as scourge of nineteenth-century European society is finished, but there is no time limit to his role as guide to the human situation. Except, perhaps, that our time is peculiarly apt for his view of it. We have been dismayed by the discovery that man is the only animal in which the fact of being crippled is almost a mark of the species. Ibsen was pointing this out a hundred years ago—and adding that the battle for survival would still go on.   ROBERT HATCH

MOVIES

Jester of the New Wave

Philippe de Broca is the Mack Sennett of the New Wave. Just as Sennett—surrounded by men making films full of villains, mortgages, and girls falling over waterfalls—staged wild encounters with pies and policemen, so does De Broca provide comedy relief in the midst of the more serious and sordid concerns of his Paris colleagues.

He was given his big opportunity by Claude Chabrol, one of the "old masters" of the New Wave. Chabrol had read a scenario submitted to him by an attractive young actress, Geneviève Cluny, and decided to produce, but not direct, it. He assigned the job of directing to De Broca, a young man (he is now twenty-eight and was, at that time, a tender twenty-six) who, until then, had been responsible for a number of short documentaries.

Two other youthful directors, François Truffaut and Jean-Luc Godard, who had helped to precipitate the New Wave in France and in this country, worked with De Broca on this film, called *The Love Game*. They both took small parts in it, too, to indicate clearly that their imprimatur was on it. Mlle Cluny, the author, won a leading role.

Chabrol (director of *Le Beau Serge, The Cousins,* and *Leda*), Truffaut (*The 400 Blows*), Godard (*Breathless*), and such other *nouvelle vaguistes* as Alain Resnais (*Hiroshima, Mon Amour*) and Louis Malle (*The Lovers*) had concentrated on serious themes. Most of us, when we see the words "New Wave," are assailed by confused memories of a number of films dealing with youth in rebellion, youth in stolen cars, and little boys running away from broken homes.* These are all excellent films, and memory has fused them into a somber cinematic plaint of anguish and despair; director De Broca has come along, it

* See "The New Wave" by Henry B. Darrach in the May, 1960, issue of HORIZON.

FRENCH FILM OFFICE

Philippe de Broca—a new René Clair?

seems, to show us that comedy, too, has a place in the Wave.

De Broca is the jester among these dark chiefs, but he is loyal; he plays his pranks, yet in every sequence of his films he also announces his devotion to their ideas. Not all their ideas are by any means new ones; film makers once knew a great many things that got lost with the introduction of sound. What the New Wave people have done is to gather together some of these ideas into their own Code Napoléon of film and use them with great skill and taste. They have discovered again, for example, that the camera can compress time and can stretch it; that a minute can be made to last an hour, and vice versa. Resnais, the maker of *Hiroshima, Mon Amour*, has shown a remarkable sensitivity to this aspect of the medium. It is also a peculiarly French concern. Because of their superior education, French film workers, no matter how avant-garde their tastes, have a sense of the cultural past that is often lacking among our own Hollywood directors and writers. Bergson and Proust, as well as the avant-garde novelist Robbe-Grillet, are part of their working heritage.

But I think that the principal and unifying characteristic of the makers of New Wave films is their knowledge (shared also by the truly modern novelists) that some things have been done so often it is not necessary to do them again. This seemingly simple insight leads to a cinematic shorthand that makes for an at first disturbing dislocation of action within a sequence. The result is nothing less than a new language of film; and it is this, not the content, that gives significance to the New Wave school. It is a form of speech from which all that is unessential has been dropped out; it is the cinematic equivalent of the linguistic devices of Icelandic sagas: a grammar without articles, a language of action; epithet is there, but not metaphor.

The New Wave film maker must ask himself such questions as: If my actor has to go from the first floor of a house to the second, must I show him walking up the stairs? His answer is No. He can cut directly from man walking toward stairs to man walking on second floor, because everyone knows what a staircase looks like and everyone knows it is necessary to climb it to reach the upper floor. The question and answer are simple, but the results are not. What it leads to are films with a constant, pulsing life; there are no pauses for unnecessary stage directions or explanations. All the directions and explanations have been made before; they can be dispensed with now.

The Love Game was a perfect little farce, a remarkably professional premier effort. It was also, in my opinion, a bit too clever; it lacked the filmic adventurousness of the best New Wave movies. It is easy enough to produce a flawless work by following the tried and true (and also untrue) methods. *The Love Game*, I think, was not so much an experimental first film as a farewell to an antique form. It was De Broca's way of showing us he could do this sort of thing as well as, or better than, anyone else.

De Broca has, in his subsequent two films—*The Joker* and *The Five-Day Lover*—turned his back on this glossy, seamless professionalism; he is no longer a director of flawless films; he stumbles, gropes, the story gets away from him. He is exploiting the medium now, pushing it, testing its limits; he is not content merely to control it like a skilled traffic policeman. De Broca knows what art is all about: it is discontent and, in his case, it is not divine but pagan.

While he has not repeated the technique of his first film, he has remained true to the philosophy enunciated there. De Broca is a passionate adherent of that school of philosophy which believes that all problems can and ought to be solved in bed. And he is a very powerful propagandist indeed: he thumps no tubs, he threatens no hell-fires; he tries to convert his audience by delighting them. And Watteau is his real master; they are both more interested in actions than in transports: to make love is more important than to love.

The Love Game deals with a young couple who work in an antique shop and live in the back, in one small room which contains, mainly, a bed. In contrast to the bedrooms of other New Wave films De Broca's are always well-lighted, charming places; they invite you; they are hard to leave. *The Love Game* begins as an idyll of unwedded bliss; it is disturbed by the girl's sudden and quite unreasonable demand that her lover marry her. He resists almost to the very end, then submits, and is last seen dancing down the street. One is left with the hopeful feeling that while marriage is clearly unnecessary, it need not always mark the end of joy.

The hero of all three of De Broca's films is a brilliant young actor named Jean-Pierre Cassel. He has a face that would delight a caricaturist: the nose is too big, the chin too small; and yet, one never doubts he is the irresistible lover and that women of great beauty

UNITED ARTISTS

Lover escapes, husband fires—and misses: Paris scene from De Broca's The Joker

would climb six flights to reach his apartment. He is the Life Force; any woman senses and finds him in the dark.

De Broca's second film, *The Joker*, opens with M. Cassel prancing across the rooftops of Paris; an irate husband is shooting at him but Cassel is not worried: he knows there are no real bullets in his world. In the course of his escape he slips into the bedroom of a beautiful woman (who also has a husband) and falls madly in love with her. He is rebuffed, but he returns (he always returns, even to the flat of the armed husband), brings flowers, disguises himself as a plumber, brush salesman, friend of the family. Finally she permits him to take her to his home. He lives with an ancient uncle, his older brother and his wife, two of his own illegitimate children (his sister-in-law may even be their mother); and with a very pretty little servant girl who comforts him when his other plans go awry.

The family is, I think, a bit fey; a little too reminiscent of the determined and stagey eccentricity of *You Can't Take It With You*. But there are marvelous scenes: Cassel playing the bassoon in the family quartet (the sister-in-law plays the drums); a jubilant

dance that De Broca raises to a fantastic pitch by playing it in fast motion. The scene recalls—and contrasts with—the boys' pillow fight in Jean Vigo's *Zero for Conduct:* the pillows tear and feathers fill the air. Suddenly Vigo switches to slow motion; what was frenetic becomes a dreamlike sequence—the feathers float languorously, the boys move with underwater grace.

De Broca's third film, *The Five-Day Lover,* is the most ambitious and the best yet. Cassel, this time, has two women. The first is a dress designer who supports him and gives him the use of her Rolls and chauffeur. The second is a married woman; her husband is an archivist who is working on a thesis that will *prove* that one Poreux did not invent the flexible joint in water pipes.

An outline of the plot could only suggest that this is yet another French bedroom farce, school of Feydeau. It is much more than that. It does not depend, as the farces do—more juggling acts than dramas—on perfectly timed entrances and exits, mistaken identities, comic disguises, and other gimmicky plot devices. If one of the French anti-novelists ever wrote a comedy, it would certainly be closer to De Broca than to De Maupassant.* The fact is, writers are not very important to the New Wave directors, even though the latter have used the services of Marguerite Duras and Robbe-Grillet.

Technically *The Five-Day Lover* is a triumphant justification of the New Wave's cinematic ideas, and of De Broca's own very personal vision. He is the master of a completely artificial "realism" which involves us directly.

To this technical mastery De Broca adds his own pagan mark. At one point in *The Five-Day Lover,* the dress designer is looking at a new bridal gown created by one of her assistants. The hem has been gathered and pulled up, fixed with a rose to reveal the bride's knee. "But is it really chaste?" she asks her assistant; and he, plump, with the face of a satyr (pre-Christian, of course) answers, "I have freed the knee for prayer."   WARREN MILLER

* See "Total Revolution in the Novel" by Richard Gilman, on page 96 of this issue.

BOOKS

Ladies Who Tell All, but All

Saint Augustine and Jean-Jacques Rousseau confessed all, or almost all, and thereby set examples of public disrobing that were to be emulated by lesser men. Yet it has not been the fashion for women—women of good repute, that is —to do likewise until now: at least not in print. True, George Sand spilled forth interminable accounts of her affairs with De Musset, Chopin, and the rest; but the predatory George, after all, was in many ways more man than woman. In a later day Isadora Duncan regaled readers of her memoirs with earthy tidbits of her nights with Gordon Craig, with a certain "Lohengrin," with a certain "Romeo," *et al.;* but Isadora, though every inch a woman, was hardly what you'd call a lady.

Today, however, gifted and personable lady writers of impeccable backgrounds have taken to delivering up their pasts to all and sundry in a manner that, if this goes on, may make even the Marquis de Sade sound tame. We have had, for instance, an American novelist, mother of two and daughter of a southern clergyman, tell the world, between book covers, all about how successful she was in helping her mortally stricken husband kill himself. We have had a prominent lady book critic, Town Hall lecturer, and arbiter of taste on some of the better television panels, address to her dead mother a 334-page diatribe designed to convey to its readers how poorly she thinks of her late mother, and of her own late husbands, too. We have had a ranking literary lioness of France provide a *roman à clef,* in which the sleeping habits and quirks of the best-known lights of her time and place are duly recorded under thin disguise, and which this spring will be followed in America by a fresh installment of her autobiography, documenting their

identities, in case there should be any doubt about them (which there isn't).

Such upper-level, artistic confessions are not to be mentioned in the same breath, of course, with those we have recently been receiving in numbers from ladies of quite another order and engaged in the pursuit of quite another form of art. Our bookstores bulge with lugubrious life-stories of the rise and fall (often several falls) of aging hetaerae, breast-beating show-business exhibitionists, and international female Casanovas, sometimes written for them by an expert sob brother. The two categories are poles apart, a chief difference between them being that when it comes to an actual episode *in flagrante,* or even in the marital couch, these authors tend to become excruciatingly reticent and prim, while the ladies of higher culture tend to become smashingly specific.

Thus, you might consult a passage on page 24 of Lael Tucker Wertenbaker's *Death of a Man;* passages on pages 127 and 128 of Virgilia Peterson's *A Matter of Life and Death;* and a wide array of passages in Simone de Beauvoir's evidently autobiographical novel, *The Mandarins,* particularly those beginning on page 341 that deal with the heroine's ardent love-life with a rising Chicago novelist.

As Virgilia Peterson puts it in her foreword, "I often wakened at night to wonder why it should be of such overwhelming moment to me to expose and explain myself"—leaving the reader of her book-length open letter to her departed mother often echoing in embarrassment, why indeed. Yet while the three authors share a consuming passion for intimate public communion, possibly for exorcism, too, their methods differ. Together they demonstrate the range of the present feminine confessional syndrome.

Mrs. Wertenbaker's might be called the hard, Hemingway memorial approach, with emphasis (all too literal, it soon turns out) on sheer blood and guts. Miss Peterson, on the other hand, works in the vein of the later Henry James, compounding her narrative with so many involved asides, unresolved self-examinations, and rhetorical obliquities that you often have trouble figuring out just where the trouble lay. Mlle de Beauvoir, meanwhile, seems determined to be the Balzac of the Café Flore—encyclopedic, remorseless, and interminable. Now fifty-three and in full literary as well as reminiscent flower, she has produced fully one thousand pages of memoirs, which, however, take her up only to her thirty-fifth year—all this in addition to her *Mandarins* (622 pages), a kind of novelistic preview which again breaks off well over a decade back—leaving an untold number of pages to go if the author is to catch up with herself today. The mind boggles at what reams may come if Françoise Sagan, too, takes to writing memoirs designed to keep pace with *her* existence.

One virtue of Mrs. Wertenbaker's approach is brevity; yet in her slender 181-page chronicle (now headed for Broadway in a stage adaptation by Garson Kanin) we are spared nothing. Its readers will recall the context of this particular passage, reminiscent in style of the master of *For Whom the Bell Tolls:* "'The hole is my friend,' Wert said, the day after he blew it. 'It's good for me.'" (It wasn't good for that brave man at all, of course; it was an erupting abdominal hemorrhage, and it signaled his doom.) But Hemingway himself never presented anything comparable to the horrendous clinical detail that Lael Wertenbaker introduces at this point. The author seems to feel that her devotion to her dying husband can best be conveyed by dwelling upon every nauseous detail of his bodily disintegration, and her version of the classic love-death motif is a triumphant climax that records her efforts in helping poor "Wert" inject death-dealing bubbles into a vein and her ministrations as he slashed his wrists. This should make a rousing hit on Broadway.

"How to write about it is a problem," she remarks at the outset of her story, speaking of a time when both partners knew what lay ahead, "because we both happened to be writing people." It never seemed to occur to her, as a writing person, that one solution might be to write about something else.

Miss Peterson, though also writing under what she calls "a high wind of compulsion," approaches the facts of life by a more circuitous route. She seems less concerned with what happened than with her own reactions to what happened—or, more often, to what didn't happen. She appears throughout her long confessional to be a woman with little, actually, to confess. True, she couldn't abide her mother and fled into her first marriage because she wanted to wed "almost as much as I wanted to leave home and you." But her successive men appear as little more than phantoms: the first is simply her "large, sandy-haired bridegroom," occupied in writing publicity for golf balls and, apart from a specific wedding-night reference, left undescribed; the second is "my Pole," "dark-eyed and slender," a prince, no less, but soon equally remote; then we have a nocturnal interlude with "the Maestro," an unnamed but readily identifiable conductor, who gave the author one of her "Life's more envenomed lessons" (though a nonvenomous reader might find the lesson slightly comic), and finally she finds solace in evening "trysts" with a "gray-haired knight-errant."

Nothing further about the golf-ball publicist, the prince, the Maestro, and the knight; but a great deal about her consistently unhappy and misunderstood self. Why unhappy? Why misunderstood? Miss Peterson, an artist with words, does not get around to explaining that. Perhaps, indeed, she has fallen victim to too much love of words—big, swooshing ones. Thus: "money as such, naked and slippery, swam up out of its shark-infested subaqueous habitat and entered my ken." Meaning? She found herself at one point short of cash.

Mlle de Beauvoir, however, is endlessly specific. She is almost Churchillian, in fact, in the scope of her memoirs. Volume one, *Memoirs of a Dutiful Daughter*, takes us only through the stringencies and frustrations of her adolescence, and ends, as a good cliffhanger should, on a strong promissory note: that is when Jean-Paul Sartre, aged twenty-one, remarks to Simone, aged nineteen, "From now on, I'm going to take you under my wing." This is her counterpart to Churchill's volume one, *The Gathering Storm;* her next (counterpart to his volume two, *Their Finest Hour*), is about to arrive, already published in France under the title *La Force de l'Age*—the finest hour in this instance being the fulfillment of Simone's and Sartre's dawning love. In its way, it parallels Churchill's *The Grand Alliance* (i.e., Sartre and Camus allied with their various friends and ladies), and presumably we shall have in due course from Mlle de Beauvoir a sequel that will be the equivalent to the Prime Minister's *Closing the Ring.*

Everything is there, in this gathering epic of café battles, of Dubonnet-aided campaigns and sexual high strategy as joined in by this most sophisticated ornament of the Boulevard St. Germain, except an answer to the question as to how sophisticated she really is. Thus, "Sexuality frightened me," she reports of her youth; then, "I had always thought very highly of love"; finally, "I want life, the whole of life."

She got "the whole of life," and no doubt is richer for it. But, being at heart simple; she can't refrain from advertising it.   WILLIAM HARLAN HALE

CHANNELS

Who Put the Alphabet into the Soup?

Someday someone must write an authoritative account of the advertising industry, from which one might learn how it began, and how it developed, and how in the name of all that's holy it managed to get where it is today. In the absence of such a volume, one must fall back on conjecture, which I shall immediately proceed to do.

Presumably, advertising began far back in prehistory when some enterprising troglodyte scribbled above his atelier, "Paleolithic Tools Made Here." (This is an extremely dubious conjecture, but it will have to do.) Obviously, such advice was of great value to the other troglodytes in the neighborhood, who knew at once where they could turn for artifacts. If the whole thing had rested there, everything might have turned out fine—which is another extremely dubious conjecture.

But in time another artificer appeared along the rialto and faced up to the problem of planning an advertising campaign of his own. After some thought, and perhaps a great deal of brainstorming, he proudly scribbled his own sign, which read *"Better* Paleolithic Tools Made Here."* That concludes the conjecture. No more is necessary. From the second of those two signs there is clearly a direct line of descent to Rosser Reeves, by way of "Milder, Much Milder," "Our Paleolithic Tools Cut Seven Ways," and "NOW! Neolithic Tools!" to Mobilgas with "Megatane Rating."

The Megatane Rating campaign irritates me (if I may borrow a technique from the Industry itself) in THREE distinct ways. Count them, THREE. In the first place, I have scrutinized all the printed and spoken material that goes with it, and I have yet to discover what it has to do with gasoline. I am never told. In the television commercials a Megatane gasoline (if that's what I mean) is compared with an octane gasoline (which doesn't convey anything), and it turns out that Mobilgas makes more circles in your engine. I am never told what the circles stand for, and I can only assume that they stand for circles. It happens I don't *want* circles in my engine—just something that will go "bang" and make the wheels turn.

In the second place, it offends the purist in me. "Octane" comes from the Spanish or Greek or Zulu or something, and the "oct-" part of it refers to the fact that somewhere or other in the gasoline there is a hydrocarbon molecule with eight carbon atoms. This is supposed to be a very good thing to have around gasoline. "Megatane," if it means anything, means a hydrocarbon molecule with a million carbon atoms, which is one hell of a molecule to have kicking around in gasoline.

I suppose that Mobilgas chose the word "megatane" because it sounds like "megaton," which has come to mean "possessing the destructive power of one million tons of TNT." I am a squeamish person, and I don't like the notion that the bright boys on Madison Avenue are busily calculating how much mileage they can get out of the hydrogen bomb. There must be other gimmicks.

As far as I am concerned, all this makes the Mobilgas people and their

agency guilty of bad taste, bad chemistry, and bad judgment, and leaves me in some doubt as to whether they make good gasoline. Well, not very much doubt; to be quite honest about it, deep down inside I am sure their gasoline is exactly the same as any other gasoline, so far as my car is concerned, and I continue to patronize the gas station with the cleanest rest rooms.

The fact that I don't like the way Mobilgas has solved its problem does not mean I am unaware of the problem's existence. It is faced by every manufacturer who produces an article identical, in all important respects, with the articles produced by the competition. He has to say *something*, damn it, and after a while the strain tells. Since he has no real handhold on the competition, he must invent one; and with the passage of time the inventions get wilder and wilder until they escape reality and soar off into non-Euclidean space.

Take the airlines, for example. The potential customer really wants to know only three things about an airline: Is it fast? Will it get him to his destination in one piece? Does it cost very much? The answers to two of these questions are quite simple but not very helpful: any airline will get him where he is going about as fast as any other, and they all cost the same. As for safety, it is a fact that some airlines are safer than others, but calling attention to it brings up a far more significant fact: the safest airline is not nearly as safe as any sober, right-thinking man would like it to be. So the airlines shrug their shoulders and make much of the food they serve, in valiant disregard of everyone's knowledge that (1) it is not the business they are in, (2) all food tastes terrible if it is served half a day after it has been cooked, and (3) man has yet to devise a more uncomfortable place to attack a full meal than in the cabin of an airplane.

This food fantasy can get entirely out of control. Some time ago in a copy of the New York *Times* I found a full-page advertisement for Lufthansa. I can't recall the details, but the impression left

by the ad was that if I flew Lufthansa I would be regally entertained in Hamburg by a Countess or Landgräfin or something. They had her picture; she looked very nice. As I have repeatedly told my wife, I fly to Hamburg because I have to fly to Hamburg, and any suggestion that I plan to dine there with a posh Countess would do me no good at home. Anyway, if she has to entertain all the people who fly Lufthansa, there must be quite a mob at the castle, and I wouldn't get much of her time. It is possible that I missed the point of the ad, which I didn't read all the way through. I may even have misunderstood it thoroughly. But if the Countess really wants to dine with me that much, she can fly over here; I can fix her up on Pan Am.

All these ventures into irrelevancy are thoroughly depressing, and the only alleviation comes from the memory of advertising campaigns that were so direct as to be unforgettable. I adduce, for example, an old campaign for Marlboro cigarettes that struck hard and to the point: "Smoke Marlboros—your friends will know they cost a few cents more." This appeal to the vulgarity that is present in all of us demonstrated a sense of reality that is no less than merciless. Actually it had a profound effect on me: I gave up smoking entirely and, with the money I saved, bought a Cézanne, which I labeled "Original Cézanne" in large yellow letters and suspended from the ceiling of my living room, where you couldn't miss it.

But, if I might fight my way back from memory lane—what would happen if some alert agency prepared a campaign which said exactly what was credible and relevant, and no more: "Use such-and-such soap—it's good," or "Buy so-and-so—$2,500's worth of automobile for $2,500." I have a suspicion that the product would sweep the market. Come to think of it, that's almost exactly what Volkswagen has done, and if it hasn't quite swept the market clean, it has cleared a nice tidy spot for itself. This may be one of those rare cases when I am right.   STEPHEN WHITE

"A Nice and Abstruse

"CHESS, *tches*, n.s.   A nice and abstruse game, in which two sets of puppets are moved in opposition to each other."
—Samuel Johnson's Dictionary, 1775

But it is *not* a game. It is a way of life in which the participant has subjected himself to a stringent intellectual discipline from childhood. It is an arena in which great intellectual feats have been accomplished, great moments of beauty created, and great passions aroused. A wrong move, a sloppy continuation, is as unpardonable and aesthetically shocking as a vulgar phrase in Mozart's *"Dove sono."* Emotions boil over. The great Aron Nimzovitch, on losing a crucial game in a tournament, mounted the table, his face purple, and yelled at the top of his voice: *"Gegen diesem Idioten muss ich verlieren!"* ("To think that I have to lose to this idiot!"). The even greater Alexander Alekhine once resigned a game by picking up his king and, frantic with rage and frustration, hurling it across the room, nearly braining a referee in the process. (Tournament pieces have bases weighted with lead; they can be dangerous weapons.)

For any artist can go mad with frustration when he finds that his conception is flawed—or, even worse, that he has ruined a brilliant conception by a stupid, obvious blunder. Artists hunt for the ideal; they spend their lives striving after a vision that no human can ever reach. No less than the other creative arts, is this true of chess, the youngest of them. It probably originated in India, whence it penetrated to Persia and Arabia. The rules then were different, though, and probably not until around the tenth century A.D. did the game solidify into a form very much like the one we know today. Theoretically, chess is pure logic. But as it is played by human beings, it is also style, imagination, psychology, and period. When two Grandmasters face each other over the board, their moves are as much determined by their personalities and the age they live in, as by the logic of the game.

Chess Review

That is why the ideal chess player would have to be a calculating machine, unmoved by emotion, with billions upon billions of moves committed to memory. For every combination there would, logically, be a refutation, and all games would necessarily end in a draw.

But that state of affairs will never come to pass, no matter how much you may read about the marvels of calculating machines. Machines cannot create, and the combinations are too fantastically complex for man or machine to master. At the end of the tenth move, so mathematicians tell us, a player can be faced with the choice of one out of 165,518,-829,100,544,000,000,000,000,000 moves. What the mathematicians do not say is that, more often than not, of that inconceivable immensity of choice, 165,518,829,100,543,-999,999,999,999,999 moves are wrong. For an error at the

Some of its masters, like composers, are classicists, others are daring romantics. And today there is an eclectic school of chess

·

Game..."

By HAROLD C. SCHONBERG

Almost all the leading chess masters of the early twentieth century met for the Grandmasters Tournament at St. Petersburg in 1914. Among those in the front row: Blackburne, Lasker, Tarrasch, Burn (second, third, fourth, fifth from the left, respectively), Rubinstein, Capablanca, and Janowski (third, second, and first from the right). Back row includes: Marshall, Alekhine, Nimzovitch (second, third, and fourth from left), and Znosko-Borovsky (far right). Lasker won the tournament; Capablanca took second prize and Alekhine third.

tenth move in master chess can mean (all other things being even) a lost game.

It can mean a lost game because several of the standard openings have been so well analyzed that the slightest misstep results in a positional flaw, which in master chess usually means a lost game. Now it may be that a computer can be programed so that it has several openings and defenses down pat. But the game is too complex for *all* openings to be programed, much less middle-game continuations. Assuming that a chess game averages out so that at every turn a player has about thirty possible meaningful moves, and that forty moves will suffice to reach a clear decision in every variation, the total number of variations to be computed would be 10 to the 120th power. So writes Dr. Edward Lasker in *The Adventure of Chess;* and he also quotes

a scientist to the effect that even if the machine could operate at one variation a micro-microsecond (one millionth of one millionth of a second), it would take 10^{90} years to calculate the first move (ten followed by ninety zeros). Thus the computer might reach the middle game in a thousand billion generations. No, computers are not ready for the job. Nor are they prepared for unpredictable moves. Computers, poor things, have no yin, no yang.

Yin and yang, Apollo and Dionysus, classic and romantic. We all have them in us, intermixed to greater or lesser degree. Part is the result of our own nature, and part is what the age tells us to be. A Bach could not have been a romantic; his age was not ready for it. But a Stravinsky can be a neoclassic. Similarly, there could have been no romanticism in the early days of chess, for romanticism was unknown anywhere in the world. But when the time was ripe, romanticism in chess appeared—as did, in turn, modernism, "hypermodernism," and eclecticism.

It is true that the theory of openings has advanced to the point where the first ten moves or so (and even the first twenty, in well-analyzed lines of play) are predetermined. A century and a half of rigorous analysis has codified the openings to the point where there are few initial surprises left. When White plays 1. P—K4 (i.e., as his opening move, his king's pawn moves two squares ahead), Black has a variety of answers. But every answer has a specific counteranswer. White immediately knows after Black's first move whether Black is going to play the French Defense, or the Sicilian, or what have you. The multiple lines of the French and the Sicilian and all the others are set down with the exactitude of logarithmic tables, and players commit them to memory. God help anybody who departs from the lines without good reason. Punishment will soon follow.

But once the opening is disposed of, the mid-game sets in,

and that is where creation enters. Also psychology, intuition, tactics, and strategy. And, once in a while, bluff. Some minds think along the lines of Apollo, some of Dionysus. The Apollonian player will strive for classicism—for simplification, for clarity, for elegance. The Dionysian will look for complications, for sacrifice and combination.

Whether romanticist or classicist, however, the great chess player is dealing with the elements of creation. Instead of notes on ruled paper, or oils, or stone, or words, he uses chess pieces. His aim is to take the raw materials and from them forge a continuity that expresses his own personality. What comes out, at its best, is on a level of expression that ordinary minds cannot match.

*T*hese are not extravagant words. In music any composer can take a given theme and develop it, but it takes a Mozart or a Beethoven to see possibilities in the theme that ordinary minds would handle only in an ordinary manner. Schubert, in the slow movement of his B flat trio, is going along in D flat and by a sudden twist ends up in the unrelated key of E major. The unexpected effect is one of sheer magic, created by sheer genius. The combination was there for all to see, but only Schubert saw it.

Similarly, any of us can push chess pieces around. But it takes an Alekhine or a Capablanca to look at a given position and see in it possibilities of continuation that are so unexpected, so beautiful, so complete in themselves, that they bring a gasp from the connoisseur. Thus in a game between Marshall and Levitzky at Breslau in 1912, when Marshall made one of the most brilliant moves in chess history (a queen sacrifice that, if accepted, would have led to mate or a shattered position) and Levitzky immediately resigned, the audience was so carried away that it is said to have showered the board with gold pieces. [The move is illustrated on the center spread of the portfolio that follows this article.]

And when Alekhine departed from "book"—that is, the normal and established sequence of a well-analyzed opening —and made his famous sixth move in the sixth game of his return championship match with Euwe, the materials were there for all to see. The position had come up thousands of times before, but Alekhine was the only one who could see the possibilities inherent in it. And so he offered the sacrifice of a knight. Euwe, gasping, took more than an hour of precious time to attempt an over-the-board analysis. The things that must have gone through his mind! Why the sacrifice? A "prepared variation"? Alekhine was not in the practice of giving presents. As Euwe looked over the board, complexity upon complexity unrolled. He did not accept the sacrifice, but was so demoralized that he lost the game.

That was in 1937, and a generation of chess analysts have pondered the position ever since. The modern consensus is that Euwe should have accepted the knight, and with careful play he would have had at least equality. But the variations are frightfully complicated and to this day have not been fully explored. Alekhine himself could not have seen every possibility. But he felt that he would have a good attack had Euwe accepted the sacrifice; he also felt that Euwe would be scared out of his wits. He was right in both instances. But what a daring and imaginative move, and what a startling departure from orthodoxy!

And that, of course, is the essence of creation: taking a situation or a set of materials available to all, and by sheer imagination and technique making it something unique and perfect, something that nobody else could duplicate.

Chess might be described as a theme (the opening) and variations (all based on the opening). But analogies between chess and music are endless. One might compare sonata form, with its exposition, development, and recapitulation, to chess, with its opening, middle game, and end game. Or take the very protagonists of the two arts and compare them. The composer reads a score like a book, away from the piano; the chess player reads *his* scores like a book, away from the board. An imaginative composer experiments with new tonal combinations; a gifted chess player experiments with new chess combinations. The composer knows the musical literature inside out; ditto the chess player with his. Ask a composer what happens in the chord that opens the last movement of the Beethoven Ninth, and he will smile and say: "Bitonal. B flat against D minor. What a conception!" Ask a chess player what happened at White's twenty-first move in the game Pillsbury-Lasker at Nuremberg in 1896, and he will smile and say: "Pawn to bishop 5, sacrificing the pawn but opening up the whole king's side and letting the knight in. What a conception!"

Even the very names of the great chess players, like those of their musical counterparts, have a rolling, resonant, unusual sound that sets them apart from other men. What an awe-inspiring ring! What majesty! Nimzovitch, Maroczy, Philidor, de la Bourdonnais, Bogolyubov, Tartakower, Botvinnik, Steinitz, Tal, Capablanca, Zukertort, Tchigorin, Reshevsky, Znosko-Borovsky. . . .

*B*oth chess and music combine the stringency of logic with the intuition of creation. Since creation enters into it, it follows that on its highest level chess would have to be a manifestation of individuality. Which it is. Any expert, glancing at a game reprinted in a magazine, can instantly tell a Réti game from a Capablanca, an Alekhine from an Euwe. Each great chess player, like each great composer, has his own style. Alekhine's has been described as "surging, restless, a combination of psychological belligerence and egoistical assurance." Euwe's is "pragmatic, mathematical, scientific, levelheaded." Capablanca's was "crystal-clear . . . as is the music of Bach." Fine's has been called "more technical than emotional." Some chess players, too, are as temperamental as Beethoven: Zukertort once sprang a surprising, devastating move against Steinitz, who stamped

*T*itans on the carpet: left, Mikhail Botvinnik, seeking to regain the world chess title he had lost the year before to Mikhail Tal (seated), paces tensely during their 1961 return match in Moscow. Then, when Botvinnik seats himself for his next move, it is Tal's turn to pace. Botvinnik won.

out of the room in a rage and never came back.

The most popular style of chess (and music and poetry, too) is the romantic, but ours is an antiromantic age and we find little romanticism these days in any of the arts. It was the great Emanuel Lasker who, in the 1880's, created modern chess and did away once and for all with pure romanticism in the game. It was in the 1880's, too, that composers like Chabrier, Strauss, and Debussy were beginning to write scores that would do away with romanticism in music. The art of chess has always followed, fairly closely, the aesthetics and stylistic periods of the other arts.

Chess had its pioneers, and Ruy Lopez in the sixteenth century was the equivalent of such composers as Giles Farnaby and John Bull. Ruy Lopez, incidentally, developed an opening that is used to the present day, one of the oldest in chess history. It goes: 1. P—K4, P—K4; 2. Kt—KB3, Kt—QB3; 3. B—Kt 5. The idea is to pin Black's queen's knight. Four hundred years of analysis in the Ruy Lopez have led to ramifications that would leave its inventor glassy-eyed.

The eighteenth century saw a revival of classicism in the arts; it entered chess at that time through the person of François André Danican Philidor (who, by the way, was an important composer of the period and the only great chess player in history to combine the two arts). Philidor, by far the best player of his day, also wrote the first important treatise on the subject, a study that was to chess almost what Bach's *Well-tempered Clavier* was to music. Both men brought order into their respective worlds. Bach's two volumes settled once and for all what the key structure of music was going to be, and Philidor's book laid down the basic rules of position play. He was the first to realize the importance of pawn structure: "The pawn is the soul of chess."

Then came the romantic period. Romanticism in chess is similar to romanticism anywhere else. It is the expression of personality; it avoids chasteness and order in favor of wild emotional gallops; it breaks rules to create new ones undreamed of by the academicians. Philidor the chess player and Haydn the composer both strove for proportion, elegance, and taste. But a player like Adolph Anderssen was the equivalent of a pianist like Liszt. Both reveled in brilliance, complexity, exhibitionism. In romantic chess the main idea is the attack. Press on! Sacrifice! Go for the jugular! It may not have been precise chess, as the classicists understood the game, and Anderssen would not have been able to take one game in fifty from today's Grandmasters. But what excitement, what flair and fireworks as the romantics disdainfully looked at their opponents and hurled combinations at them!

Many of Anderssen's games can be replayed with enjoyment today. They are masterpieces, and some have been given names: the "Evergreen," the "Immortal." But Anderssen and others of the romantic school did not have a chance when the young players who started the modern school came along. The first was an American, Paul Morphy. He was a chess prodigy who developed into a great player. (Chess has had four outstanding prodigies in its history—Morphy, Capablanca, Reshevsky, and Bobby Fischer, who won the United States championship four years ago at the age of fourteen and has retained it ever since.) Morphy came up out of New Orleans, beat everybody in America, and went to Europe where he easily trounced Anderssen. Nobody in the world at that time, 1858, could stand up to him. In Paris he beat the entire Versailles Chess Club, they playing in consultation against him while he was blindfolded. (Blindfold chess is a stunt in which a player takes on one or more opponents without being allowed to look at the board. He carries all of the games in his head. Not too long ago Miguel Najdorf of Argentina set the world's record for simultaneous blindfold play—forty-five boards at one time.)

Morphy was successful because he realized that a flashy but unsound combination would founder against an accurate defense. He was the pioneer of positional play. Set up a sound position, he said, and the rest would take care of itself; development was more important than premature attack. Thus, where the romantics would rush out with their heavy pieces, advancing them ahead of the pawns, Morphy would bide his time, like a general attending to his fortifi-

Two American chess prodigies: Samuel Reshevsky is seen (left) in 1920, when he was already a great player, aged nine; Bobby Fischer (right) in 1959, a year after he had become the U. S. champion at fourteen. Reshevsky held the championship from 1936 to 1944; Fischer holds it now.

cations. The enemy would batter himself against a solid foundation of pawns and minor pieces; and then, the enemy's power spent, Morphy would counterattack, always successfully. He was one of the first of the eclectics in chess, in that his romanticism was tempered by a strong streak of classicism.

William Steinitz, the first world champion (1866), followed Morphy's precepts. But he was even more of an antiromantic. Playing slowly, laboriously, and tenaciously, he built to a sound position against which the romantics shattered themselves. Rather than lead with his chin or make the flashy gesture, he strove always for an accumulation of small advantages. These tiny footholds he would build up to an overwhelming position, and his aghast opponents would see their games literally melt away.

With Emanuel Lasker, who succeeded Steinitz in 1894, modern chess really came into being. He added something new—psychological chess. His opponents called it luck and wondered how he could continue to win in positions that were manifestly "unsound." They did not realize that Lasker purposely made unsound moves to draw his opponents on. He studied all his competitors microscopically—their games, their style, their idiosyncrasies, their strong and weak points. He was not so much interested in making the best moves as in making those most disagreeable to his opponents. Always he managed to turn the game into lines that made them squirm, relying on his tactical genius to keep himself out of trouble.

But youth must be served. After holding the title for twenty-seven years, Lasker surrendered it to Capablanca in 1921—Capablanca, who deservedly may be called the Mozart of chess; the greatest natural player who ever lived;

the player with instinct rather than learning; the genius who could glance at a position and see more than other masters could analyze in a month. Only a supreme player could have dethroned him, and a supreme player did, in 1927.

In the Russian-born Alexander Alekhine all styles fused. He could be as classic as Capablanca, as modern as Lasker, as romantic as Anderssen, as hypermodern as Réti or Nimzovitch. (The "Hypermoderns," after the First World War, were analogous to a composer like Schoenberg—iconoclastic, frequently bizarre, full of new theories.) But Alekhine was neither a pedant nor an eclectic. He was brilliant, dynamic, artistic (in his personal life he was less attractive: completely amoral, an alcoholic, an alleged worker for the Nazis). But amoral or not, he lived for nothing but chess. Every day he spent from four to eight hours at it, analyzing games and openings, looking for improvements and new ideas. To prepare himself for his match with Capablanca he went into training. He stopped drinking and smoking, got plenty of exercise and sleep, studied theory, and memorized all of the Capablanca games. No player in history had such a ferocious will to win.

Alekhine was a supreme virtuoso. His best period gave to the world a brilliant series of bold, energetic, imaginative games. Tension was piled upon tension. Unheard-of complications were built up. His opponents seldom could analyze an Alekhine position over the board.

He was the last great personality in chess, although two youngsters—Bobby Fischer, from America, and Mikhail Tal, the young Russian who held the world's championship for a year—may bring back a romantic quality that will excite the public. Alekhine's three successors, up to Tal, were eclectics, and their style never captured the public imagination as did the games of Capablanca and Alekhine. Max Euwe, Mikhail Botvinnik, and Vassily Smyslov were, and are, tremendous players, but they are more like depersonalized calculating machines than anything else. Many of today's players, like many of today's composers, are of that school—all memory and technique, with relatively little personality, and loath to take a chance. Many chess lovers feel that the modern champions have taken the romance out of chess, as (some feel) composers like Hindemith, Petrassi, Babbitt, and Boulez have taken the romance out of music.

But today's players require memory and technique. They have to study games and theory the way a doctor keeps up with his medical journals or a musician with new scores. The parallels are exact. Chess has not only a venerable and fantastic literature, but also an ever-growing one. In the pockets of a chess master are stuffed current copies of the *Chess Review* from America and its counterparts from England, France, Russia, and Yugoslavia, which all publish reports of new games on the international front, complete with analyses. These are the bread and butter, the food and drink, of the chess player—these and combination studies, end-game studies, mid-game studies, *Modern Chess Open-*

ings, Alekhine's *My Best Games of Chess,* Capablanca's *My Best Games of Chess,* Lasker's *My Best Games of Chess,* everybody's *My Best Games of Chess.*

For theory has advanced to the point where memory, as well as intuition and genius, plays a major part. Thus in the 1959 United States championship tournament Fischer was playing Reshevsky in a crucial game. Here was the veteran Samuel Reshevsky, old, as chess players go (in his forties), the most highly rated player outside the Iron Curtain, an eclectic performer with a formidable feeling for position play and an icy determination to win. Here was young Fischer, only sixteen, cocky and even arrogant, perhaps (with the exception of Capablanca) the greatest natural genius chess ever produced, with a will to win as great as Reshevsky's, and with a more romantic, devil-may-care attitude toward the game. Fischer played White in a Sicilian Defense. At a certain position he remembered an analysis he had seen in a French magazine. Several moves later Reshevsky was without a queen; he struggled for twenty more moves or so, but it was hopeless.

That is why youth has the advantage in chess. There is much to memorize, and a young brain can retain more. Also a young body has more stamina and reacts better under the anguish of time pressure. Tournament or match play is a young man's game. Players have been known to drop fifteen pounds during the course of a tournament. The mental strain of five daily hours of fierce concentration takes its physical toll. Most tournament chess gives each player two and a half hours to make forty moves and is played with a double clock before the opponents. When one player makes a move he simultaneously bangs a lever that stops his clock and starts his opponent's. The clocks are preset so that a little flag on each face falls when two and a half hours are up. If a flag falls before the fortieth move, the player who belongs to that clock automatically loses the game, even though he may be ahead in material and is about to mate on the next move. As often as not, a player finds himself with one minute in which to make twenty or so

moves. This is known as time pressure. And after the game the player spends sleepless nights analyzing adjourned positions, and when he is not analyzing, he is brooding over lost games that he should have won. All of this takes it out of a man. When Lasker, at the age of sixty-seven, played through nineteen rounds in a tough Russian tournament, finishing third, his feat was described as a biological miracle.

Generally a great player reaches his peak in his thirties. After that, although he will always remain a formidable opponent, deterioration begins to set in. Most of the great players have made their mark in tournament play before reaching the age of twenty. If they haven't made it by then, they never will.

Youth seems to have an advantage in intuition, which is so important in chess. In a complicated position no brain can analyze the variations over the board—not with the clock ticking away. But where analysis fails, intuition can step in. The master *feels,* on the basis of his experience and instinct, a certain move will turn out well. He makes it, and generally he is right. Psychologists call this preconscious calculation. Whatever it is, no important chess player lacks it.

A good and patient analyst will devote years to studying games and openings. In analyzing the various lines of play he may come up with discoveries of his own. These he may hold, waiting for the proper time and place. The experts call these secret weapons "prepared variations." Marshall once saved a move for ten years and sprang it against Capablanca. But alas! the genius of Capablanca solved the move over the board, refuted it, and Marshall lost. Harry Nelson Pillsbury, the brilliant American player of the 1890's, held a move for quite a few years because he wanted to revenge himself on Lasker. The two finally met in St. Petersburg. Pillsbury swung the opening into the lines he wanted, hit Lasker with the move, and won the game.

In 1945 the USSR held a radio match with the United States. Reshevsky, then at the height of his powers, played Smyslov, and at the twenty-third move found himself in a precarious position. Reshevsky was playing the black pieces

STATEMENT REQUIRED BY THE ACT OF AUGUST 24, 1912, AS AMENDED BY THE ACTS OF MARCH 3, 1933, JULY 2, 1946, AND JUNE 11, 1960 (74 Stat. 208) SHOWING THE OWNERSHIP, MANAGEMENT, AND CIRCULATION OF HORIZON, published bi-monthly at New York, N. Y. for October 1, 1960.

1. The names and addresses of the publisher, editor, and managing editor are: Publisher, James Parton, Editor, William Harlan Hale, Managing Editor, Eric Larrabee; all of 551 Fifth Avenue, New York 17, N. Y.

2. The owner is: American Heritage Publishing Co., Inc., 551 Fifth Avenue, New York 17, N. Y.; stockholders owning or holding 1 per cent or more of total amount of stock: American Association for State and Local History, Sturbridge, Mass.; The Society of American Historians, Inc., Princeton Library, Princeton, N. J.; Charles Bruce Catton; Irwin Glusker; Oliver O. Jensen; Frank H. Johnson; Richard M. Ketchum; James Parton, individually and as Trustee under Declaration of Trust for James Parton III, dated 12/30/57, as Trustee under Declaration of Trust for Dana Parton, dated 12/30/57 and as Trustee under Declaration of Trust for Agnes L. Parton and a Child of the Grantor, dated 11/15/58; Gerald P. Rosen; Joseph J. Thorndike, Jr., individually and as Trustee under Declaration of Trust for John Thorndike, dated 12/27/57, as Trustee under Declaration of Trust for Alan Thorndike, dated 12/27/57, and as Trustee under Declaration of Trust for Anna Beardsley Lemont, dated 9/15/58; all of 551 Fifth Avenue, New York 17, N. Y.; Richard V. Benson, 301 East 47th Street, New York, N. Y.; Alexander Hehmeyer, 575 Madison Avenue, New York 22, N. Y.; E. F. Hutton & Co. for Margery F. Sachs, 61 Broadway, New York 6, N. Y.; Arnold H. Maremont, 168 North Michigan Ave., Chicago 1, Ill.; A. J. Ostheimer III, 1510 Chestnut Street, Philadelphia 2, Pa.; E. Michele Phillips, P. O. Box 11, Rowayton, Conn.; Roger S. Phillips, P. O. Box 11, Rowayton, Conn.; Cecily Sachs, c/o Bankers Trust Co., P. O. Box 704, Church Street Station, New York 8, N. Y.; E. J. Stackpole, 220 Telegraph Building, Harrisburg, Pa.; Barbara Joan Straus, 303 St. Pierre Road, Los Angeles 24, Cal.

3. The known bondholders, mortgagees, and other security holders owning or holding 1 per cent or more of total amount of bonds, mortgages, or other securities are: None.

4. Paragraphs 2 and 3 include, in cases where the stockholder or security holder appears upon the books of the company as trustee or in any other fiduciary relation, the name of the person or corporation for whom such trustee is acting; also the statements in the two paragraphs show the affiant's knowledge and belief as to the circumstances and conditions under which stockholders and security holders who do not appear upon the books of the company as trustees, hold stock and securities in a capacity other than that of a bona fide owner.

5. The average number of copies of each issue of this publication sold or distributed, through the mails or otherwise, to paid subscribers during the 12 months preceding the date shown above was: 159,525.

Signed, James Parton, Publisher. Sworn to and subscribed before me this 6th day of September, 1961. [SEAL] Lawrence P. Sweeney, Notary Public (my commission expires March 30, 1962).

in a Ruy Lopez opening, and he had taken an hour and a half up to that point. Reshevsky knew the opening lines as well as anybody alive, or thought he did. Anyway, at his twenty-third move the American team radioed for the time consumed by Smyslov. Back came the answer: one minute. When Reshevsky learned that Smyslov had taken only sixty seconds for his first twenty-three moves, he knew he was up against a prepared variation. He could not solve it over the board. Later it was learned that the whole variation had been published earlier that year in a Soviet magazine. Smyslov had it down cold.

*S*tudies have been made of the great chess players. What makes them tick? What does one need to be a Morphy or an Alekhine? No answers have been forthcoming. Great chess players, like great scientists or literary figures or musicians, come from everywhere—from rich families and from poor families; from the upper, middle, and lower classes. Some have high IQ's, and some do not appear to be especially bright. Some, like Alekhine, have no interests outside of chess. Some, like Johannes Zukertort, have interests that are fabulously varied.

Zukertort died in 1889 at the age of forty-six. In those forty-six years he managed to master eight or nine languages and acquire a working knowledge of Turkish, Arabian, and Sanskrit, to write learned articles on philosophy and theology, and to become one of the pioneer social scientists. As a young man he studied piano with none other than the great Ignaz Moscheles (the pianist-composer and the teacher of Mendelssohn), and from 1862 to 1866 he was the music critic for a Silesian newspaper. In 1865 he took his M.D. degree, with a specialty in chemistry and physiology. He edited a leading political journal of the day and also wrote articles for Bismarck's *Allegemeine Zeitung,* as well as being a foreign correspondent for that publication. An expert swordsman and pistol shot, he was a military hero, with nine decorations for bravery under fire. Once he was left for dead on the field of battle. He edited the *Berliner Schach-Zeitung* and the *Chess Monthly.* As a chess player he was ranked No. 2 in the world for many years. In his day he broke the world's record for blindfold play by taking on sixteen players. Twice he met Steinitz for the world's championship. The first time, in 1871, he was beaten. A return match took place in 1886 in America. Zukertort was trounced so badly that his spirit was broken; he died three years later.

Not all chess players have such fabulous careers or such superior intellectual endowments. But certain things all great chess players have in common—a superior memory, intense powers of concentration, strong nerves, physical stamina, and creative ability. Many are complete egocentrics. "When I play White I win because I have the first move," said Bogulyubov. "When I play Black I win because I am Bogulyubov."

Alekhine had this egocentricity above all others. He *knew* he was better than anybody else, and the will to win was paramount in his nature. Steinitz also had it in good measure. He hated to give up a game. Often he would simply wear down the opposition, fighting it out even when the position seemed a dead draw. The Germans call this *Totsitzen*—to outsit your opponent until he drops dead. Capablanca never had this kind of determination. He was invincible for many years; but had he also possessed Alekhine's competitive spirit, he would have been the greatest player who ever lived.

Nerves, or the lack of them, play a part in master chess. Some players get rattled under time pressure and make mistakes that even a *Patzer* (the chess term for a duffer) would avoid. Most experts believe that Akiba Rubinstein would easily have become world's champion had he not suffered so from nerves. He had a tendency to blow up under time pressure. An icebox like Reshevsky, in his great days, never seemed disturbed by the clock. A gnome of a man with a bulging bald head, he would sit there like an automaton. He took plenty of time and generally found himself with twenty-five moves to go and only five minutes in which to make them. Then bang! bang! bang! Calmly moving his pieces with infinite precision and speed, he would leave the kibitzers, and generally his opponent, far behind. When the smoke cleared, he had a won game.

In a way, Reshevsky's style has been typical of modern chess. Present-day players tend to be eclectic. They like complicated positions and, as did Lasker, play for tiny advantages. They seize on the small mistakes of their opponents and slowly turn them to their own positional advantage. One simply cannot afford to make a tiny mistake or miscalculation against them. A game may last forty or fifty moves; but a minute positional advantage at the fifteenth move means the game, and both players know it.

Brilliancies in modern chess are getting fewer and fewer as the level of play and theory gets higher and higher. Today's chess has been derided as cut and dried—all technique, book knowledge, and memory. And it is true that the modern players do pack in their heads a fantastic amount of "book." But, as the music and art critics constantly observe, technique is only a means to an end, not the end itself. It all depends on the players, and there are a few around who conceivably could pick up where Alekhine left off. One of these days Tal the Russian and Fischer the American, both young, both vital, both full of ideas and imagination, are going to sit facing each other across the chessboard, the world's championship at stake. Both are great technicians, both take chances, both are attacking players; and once again the romance of chess will live.

Harold C. Schonberg, the music critic of the New York Times, *is a member of the Manhattan Chess Club, in good standing but "with no rating—I came to the game too late."*

OPPOSITE: METROPOLITAN MUSEUM OF ART, GIFTS OF THE BERTHA KING BENKARD MEMORIAL FUND, 1946 AND GUSTAVAS A. PFEIFFER, 1948, 1953; SPREAD I: METROPOLITAN MUSEUM OF ART, GIFT OF GUSTAVAS A. PFEIFFER, 1948; SPREAD II: SET: MUSEUM OF NATURAL HISTORY; BOARD: CARLEBACH GALLERY; SPREAD III: METROPOLITAN MUSEUM OF ART, GIFT OF GUSTAVAS A. PFEIFFER, 1948; BOTTOM RIGHT: COURTESY THE DONALD M. LIDDELL COLLECTION; LAST PAGE: CARLEBACH GALLERY

A PRIDE
OF
CHESSMEN

Though encrusted with tradition, chess encourages originality in its devotees—as in the numberless artists who have designed their own variations of its classic pieces, often with fantastic results. Here HORIZON presents a portfolio of some of the most exuberant, from many a time and place, photographed by Lee Boltin. Below, dominated by a fanciful nineteenth-century Indian king in ivory (foreground), there stand, from left, figures in silver (English), wood (American, contemporary), jasper ware (Wedgwood, c. 1830), gold filigree (Maltese), enameled ivory (Indian), colored ivory (Burmese, perhaps seventeenth-century).

Workers vs. Czarists. A Soviet Russian set in porcelain (fired at the former Imperial works near Leningrad) applies Marxism to the game and converts it into a class struggle. Opposite, the Red king and queen are triumphant proletarians; the bishop is a Red soldier, the rook an anvil. This page, the White king wears a death's head; figure pieces caricature the old regime; the pawn is enchained.

England vs. France. In a nineteenth-century English set of silver and silver gilt entitled "The Field of the Cloth of Gold," England (opposite) is led by King Henry VIII, supported by a still unbeheaded queen and a cleric who resembles Cardinal Wolsey. France is led by Francis I, and the bishop suggests Chancellor Antoine Duprat. Such ornamental sets are avoided by chess masters as too distracting.

No single chess piece has aroused more creative imagination around the globe than that powerful end-game figure, the rook—as this sampler of ten unique designs attests. They range over many cultures and generations, each artist being lord of his own castle.

Left, Gothic-style fortress from the "Cloth of Gold" set shown earlier in this portfolio; right, in sequence, Burmese temple rook (ivory); silver tower mounted on a rhinoceros (English, George III); Sèvres porcelain figure resembling a salt shaker, after a design by Lalique (French, 1920's); Wedgwood design in the form of an old lookout tower (jasper ware).

Left, painted ivory rook from an early nineteenth-century set made in India, where traditionally the piece is given the shape of a boat; right, flamboyant late Empire Austrian piece (agate and carnelian, with inset jewels); primitive piece from present-day Nigeria (natural and stained wood); nineteenth-century Russian rook, following a medieval design and representing a galleon (walrus ivory); French vaselike innovation (faïence, contemporary).

A duplicate of this sculpture, five
and a half inches high, of
heavy steel surfaced with enamel,
was recently bought by New
York's Museum of Modern Art.
Its maker, the Catalan-born
American artist Joan Junyer, de-
scribes it also as a "free-standing
painting." Actually it is a piece
for a chess set designed by Junyer
in 1954—a rook, no less.